Top Rated™ Paddling Adventures

Top Rated™ Paddling Adventures

Canoeing, Kayaking & Rafting in North America

Edited by
Maurizio Valerio

THE DERRYDALE PRESS
Lanham and New York

THE DERRYDALE PRESS

Published in the United States of America
by The Derrydale Press
4720 Boston Way, Lanham, Maryland 20706

Distributed by NATIONAL BOOK NETWORK, INC.

Artwork by Steamroller Studios; Cover art by Fifth Street Design; Maps by Map Art, Cartesia Software; Cartoons by Tom Novak, Novak Studio.

ISBN: 1-58667-005-0 (paperback : alk. paper)
Library of Congress Card Number: 00-102311

Please note: Picked-By-You LLC and the editor have used their best efforts in preparing this book as an all-encompassing authority on the outdoors. This book was developed as a consumer guide for the outdoor enthusiast. All outdoor professionals and businesses featured in this book were selected by their past clients, according to the rules explained in the book. Picked-By-You LLC and the editor make no representation with regard to the past and/or future performance of the outdoor professionals and businesses listed. Picked-By-You LLC and the editor make no warranties with respect to the accuracy or completeness of the contents of this book, and specifically disclaim any implied warranties, merchantability, or fitness for any particular purpose and shall in no event be liable for any injury, loss of profit or any other commercial damage, including but not limited to special, incidental, consequential, or other damages.

To Allison, Marco and Nini

Table of Contents

Table of Contents

Top Rated™
Paddling Adventures

Acknowledgments

It is customary in this section to give credit to those who have contributed to the realization of the end product. The Top Rated™ Guides started three years ago as a little personal crusade and has evolved into a totally challenging, stimulating and rewarding full time commitment.

My deep thanks must go first to all the Captains, Ranchers, Guides, Lodges and Outfitters who decided to trust our honesty and integrity. They have taken a leap of faith in sharing their lists of clients with us and for this we are truly honored and thankful.

They have constantly encouraged our idea. Captains have taught us the difference between skinny fishing and skinny dipping, while River Guides have patiently helped us to identify rafters, purlins, catarafts and J-rig rafts. They were also ready to give us a badly needed push forward every time this very time-consuming idea came to a stall. We have come to know many of them through pleasant phone chats, e-mails, faxes and letters. They now sound like old friends on the phone and we are certain we all share a deep respect for the mountains, the deserts and the waters of this great country of ours.

The Top Rated Team (both in the office and abroad), with months of hard work, skills, ingenuity, good sense of humor and pride, have then transformed a simple good idea into something a bit more tangible and much more exciting. They all have put their hearts in the concept and their hands and feet in the dirt. Some with a full-time schedule, some with a part-time collaboration, all of them bring their unique and invaluable style and contribution.

My true thanks to Brent Beck, Lindsay Benson, Robert Evans, Cheryl Fisher, Brian Florence, Slim Olsen, Grace Martin, Kevin McNamara, Jerry Meek, Allison C. Mickens, Tom Novak, Shelby Sherrod, Giuseppe Verdi and Mr. Peet's Coffee and Tea.

Last, but not least, my sincere, profound, and loving gratitude to my wife Allison. Her patient support, her understanding, her help and her skills have been the fuel which started and stoked this fire. Her laughter has been the wind to fan it.

To you, Allison, with a toast to the next project…just kidding!

Maurizio Valerio

Preface

The value of information depends on its usefulness. Simply put, whatever allows you to make informed choices will be to your advantage. To that end, Top Rated™ Guides aims to take the guesswork out of selecting services for outdoor activities. Did you get what you paid for? From Top Rated™ Guides' point of view, the most reliable indicator is customer satisfaction.

The information in this book is as reliable as those who chose to participate. In the process of selecting the top professionals, Top Rated™ Guides contacted all licensed guides, outfitters and businesses which provide services for outdoor activities. They sought to include everyone but not all who were contacted agreed to participate according to the rules. Thus, the omission of a guide, outfitter or service does not automatically mean they didn't qualify based on customer dissatisfaction.

The market abounds with guidebooks by 'experts' who rate a wide range of services based on their personal preferences. The value of the Top Rated concept is that businesses earn a place in these books only when they receive favorable ratings from a majority of clients. If ninety percent of the customers agree that their purchase of services met or exceeded their expectations, then it's realistic to assume that you will also be satisfied when you purchase services from the outdoor professionals and businesses included in this book.

It's a fact of life; not everyone is satisfied all of the time or by the same thing. Individual experiences are highly subjective and are quite often based on expectations. One person's favorable response to a situation might provoke the opposite reaction in another. A novice might be open to any experience without any preconceived notions while a veteran will be disappointed when anything less than great expectations aren't met.

If you select any of the businesses in this book, chances are excellent that you will know what you are buying. A diversity of clients endorsed them because they believed the services they received met or exceeded their expectations. Top Rated™ Guides regards that information as more valuable than a single observer or expert's point of view.

The intent behind Top Rated™ Guides is to protect the consumer from being misled or deceived. It is obvious that these clients were given accurate information which resulted in a positive experience and a top rating. The number of questionnaire responses which included detailed and sometimes lengthy comments impressed upon us the degree to which people value their experiences. Many regard them as "once-in-a-lifetime" and "priceless," and they heaped generous praise on those whose services made it possible.

Top Rated™ Guides has quantified the value of customer satisfaction and created a greater awareness of top-rated outdoor professionals. It remains up to you to choose and be the judge of your own experience. With the help of this book, you will have the advantage of being better informed when making that pick.

Robert Evans, *information specialist*

The Top Rated™ Concept

Mission Statement

The intent of this publication is to provide the outdoor enthusiast and his/her family with an objective and easy-to-read reference source that would list only those businesses and outdoor professionals who have **agreed to be rated** and have been overwhelmingly endorsed by their past clients.

There are many great outdoor professionals (Guides, Captains, Ranches, Lodges, Outfitters) who deserve full recognition for putting their experience, knowledge, long hours, and big hearts into this difficult job. With this book we want to reward those deserving professionals while providing an invaluable tool to the general public.

Top Rated™ Guides are the only consumer guides to outdoor activities.

In this respect it would be useful to share the philosophy of our Company, succinctly illustrated by our Mission Statement:

> "To encourage and promote the highest professional and ethical standards among those individuals, Companies, Groups or Organizations who provide services to the Outdoor Community.
>
> To communicate and share the findings and values of our research and

surveys to the public and other key groups.

To preserve everyone's individual right of a respectful, knowledgeable and diversified use of our Outdoor Resources."

Our business niche is well defined and our job is simply to listen carefully.

THEY "the Experts" versus WE "the People"

Top Rated books were researched and compiled by **asking people such as yourself**, who rafted, fished, hunted or rode a horse on a pack trip with a particular outdoor professional or business, to rate their services, knowledge, skills and performance.

Only the ones who received A- to A+ scores from their clients are found listed in these pages.

The market is flooded with various publications written by 'experts' claiming to be the ultimate source of information for your vacation. We read books with titles such as <u>The Greatest River Guides</u>, <u>The Complete Guide to the Greatest Fishing Lodges</u>, etc.

We do not claim to be experts in any given field, but we rather pass to history as good....listeners. In the preparation of the Questionnaires we listened first to the outdoor professionals' point of view and then to the comments and opinions of thousands of outdoor enthusiasts. We then organized the findings of our research and surveys in this and other publications of this series.

Thus we will not attempt to tell you how to fish, how to paddle or what to bring on your trip. We are leaving this to the outdoor professionals featured in this book, for they have proven to be outstanding in providing much valuable information before, during and after your trip.

True [paid] advertising: an oxymoron

Chili with beans is considered a redundant statement for the overwhelming majority of cooks but it is an insulting oxymoron for any native Texan.

In the same way, while 'true paid advertising' is a correct statement for some, it is a clear contradiction in terms for us and certainly many of you. A classic oxymoron.

This is why we do not accept commissions, donations, invitations, or, as many publishers cleverly express it, "...extra fees to help defray the cost of publication". Many articles are written every month in numerous specialized magazines in which the authors tour the country from lodge to lodge and camp to camp sponsored, invited, or otherwise compensated in many different shapes or forms.

It is indeed a form of direct advertising and, although this type of writing usually conveys a good amount of general information, in most cases it lacks the impartiality so valuable when it comes time to make the final selection for your vacation or outdoor adventure.

Without belittling the invaluable job of the professional writers and their integrity, we decided to approach the task of **researching information and sharing it with the public** with a different angle and from an opposite direction.

Money? ... No thanks!

We are firmly **committed to preserve the impartiality** and the novelty of the Top Rated idea.

For this reason we want to reassure the reader that the outdoor professionals and businesses featured in this book have not paid (nor will they pay), any remuneration to Top Rated™ Guides or the editor in the form of money, invitations or any other considerations.

They have earned a valued page in this book solely as the result of *their hard work and dedication to their clients.*

"A spot in this book cannot be purchased: it must be earned"

Size of a business is not a function of its performance

Since the embryonic stage of the Top Rated idea, during the compilation of the first Top Rated book, we faced a puzzling dilemma.

Should we establish a minimum number of clients under which a business or outdoor professional will not be allowed to participate in our evaluating process?

This would be a 'safe' decision when it comes the time to elaborate the responses of the questionnaires. But we quickly learned that many outdoor professionals limit, by choice, the total number of clients and, by philosophy of life, contain and control the size of their business. They do not want to grow too big and sacrifice the personal touches or the freshness of their services. In their words "we don't want to take the chance to get burned out by people." They do not consider their activity just a job, but rather a way of living.

"WHY, NO MAM, WE NEVER HAVE HAD ANY OF THOSE SASQUATCH SIGHTINGS IN THESE PARTS."

But if this approach greatly limits the number of clients accepted every year we must say that these outdoor professionals are the ones who often receive outstanding ratings and truly touching comments from their past clients.

Some businesses have provided us with a list of clients of 40,000, some with 25 . In this book **you will find both the large and the small**.

From a statistical point, it is obvious that a fly fishing guide who submitted a list of 32 clients, by virtue of the sample size of the individuals surveyed, will implicitly have a lower level of accuracy if compared to a business for which we surveyed 300 guests. (Please refer to the Rating and Data Elaboration Sections for details on how we established the rules for qualification and thus operated our selection.)

We do not believe that the size of business is a function of its good performance and we feel strongly that those dedicated professionals who choose to remain small deserve an equal chance to be included.

We tip our hats

We want to recognize all the Guides, Captains, Ranches, Lodges and Outfitters who have participated in our endeavor, whether they qualified or not. The fact alone that they accepted to be rated by their past clients is a clear indication of how much they care, and how willing they are to make changes.

We also want to credit all those outdoor enthusiasts who have taken the time to complete the questionnaires and share their memories and impressions with us and thus with you. Some of the comments sent to us were hilarious, some were truly touching.

We were immensely pleased by the reaction of the outdoor community at large. The idea of "Top Rated™ Guides" was supported from the beginning by serious professionals and outdoor enthusiasts alike. We listened to their suggestions, their comments, their criticisms and we are now happy to share this information with you.

Questionnaires

"Our books will be only as good as the questions we ask."

We posted this phrase in the office as a reminder of the importance of the 'tool' of this trade. The questions.

Specific Questionnaires were tailored to each one of the different activities surveyed for this series of books. While a few of the general questions remained the same throughout, many were specific to particular activities. The final objective of the questionnaire was to probe the many different facets of that diversified field known as the outdoors.

The first important factor we had to consider in the preparation of the Questionnaires was the total number of questions to be asked. Research shows an *inversely proportionate relation* between the total number of questions and the percentage of responses: the higher the number of questions, the lower the level of response. Thus we had to balance an acceptable return rate with a meaningful significance. We settled for a compromise and we decided to keep 20 as the maximum number.

The first and the final versions of the Questionnaires on which we based our surveys turned out to be very different. We asked all the businesses and outdoor professionals we contacted for suggestions and criticisms. They helped us a great deal: we weighed their different points of view and we incorporated all their suggestions into the final versions.

We initially considered using a phone survey, but we quickly agreed with the businesses and outdoor professional that we all are already bothered by too many solicitation calls when we are trying to have a quiet dinner at home. We do not want you to add Top Rated to the list of companies that you do not want to talk to, nor do we want you to add our 800 number to your caller ID black list.

In using the mail we knew that we were going to have a slightly lower percentage of questionnaires answered, but this method is, in our opinion, a more respectful one.

We also encouraged the public to participate in the designing of the questionnaire by posting on our website at www.topratedsurveys.com the opportunity to submit a question and ...."Win a book". Many sent their suggestions and, if they were chosen to be used in one of our questionnaires, they were given the book of their choice.

Please send us your question and/or your suggestions for our future surveys to:

Top Rated™ Surveys, P.O. Box 718, Baker City, OR 97814

Rating (there is more than one way to skin the cat)

We considered many different ways to score the questionnaires, keeping in mind at all times our task:

translate an opinion into a numerical value

Some of the approaches considered were simple *averages* [arithmetical means], others were sophisticated statistical tests. In the end we opted for simplicity, sacrificing to the God of statistical significance. WARNING: if $p \leq 0.001$ has any meaning in your life stop reading right here: you will be disappointed with the rest.

For the rest of us, we also made extensive use in our computation of the *median*, a statistic of location, which divides the frequency distribution of a set of data into two halves. A quick example, with our imaginary Happy Goose Outfitter, will illustrate how in many instances the *median* value, being the center observation, helps in describing the distribution, which is the truly weak point of the *average*:

Average salary at Happy Goose Outfitters $ 21,571

Median salary at Happy Goose Outfitters $ 11,000

5,000	10,000	10,000	11,000	12,000	15,000	98,000
Wrangler	Guide	Guide	Senior Guide	Asst.Cook	Cook	Boss

Do not ask the boss : "What's the average salary?"

These are the values assigned to **Questions 1-15**:

5.00 points	OUTSTANDING
4.75 points	EXCELLENT
4.25 points	GOOD
3.50 points	ACCEPTABLE
3.00 points	POOR
0.00 points	UNACCEPTABLE

Question 16, relating to the weather conditions, was treated as bonus points to be added to the final score.

Good=0   Fair=1   Poor=2

The intention here was to reward the outdoor professional who had to work in adverse weather conditions.

Questions 17 - 18 = 5 points

Questions 19 - 20 = 10 points

The individual scores of each Questionnaire were expressed as a percentage to avoid the total score from being drastically affected by one question left unanswered or marked "not applicable." All the scores received for each individual outdoor professional and business were thus added and computed.

The 90 points were considered our cutoff point. Note how the outfitters must receive a combination of Excellent with only a few Good marks (or better) in order to qualify.

Only the Outfitters, Captains, Lodges, Guides who received an A- to A+ score did qualify and they are featured in this book.

We also decided not to report in the book pages the final scores with which the businesses and the outdoor professionals ultimately qualified. In a way we thought that this could be distractive.

In the end, we must admit, it was tough to leave out some outfitters who scored very close to the cutoff mark.

It would be presumptuous to think that our scoring system will please everybody, but we want to assure the reader that we tested different computations of the data. We feel the system that we have chosen respects the overall opinion of the guest/client and maintains a more than acceptable level of accuracy.

We know that .... "You can change without improving, but you cannot improve without changing."

The Power of Graphs (how to lie by telling the scientific truth)

The following examples illustrate the sensational (and unethical) way with which the 'scientific' computation of data can be distorted to suit one's needs or goals.

The *Herald* presents a feature article on the drastic increase of total tonnage of honey stolen by bears (mostly Poohs) in a given area during 1997.

Total tonnage of honey stolen by bears (Poohs)

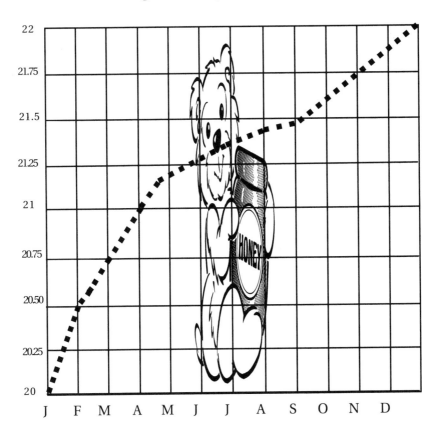

Total tonnage of honey stolen by bears (Poohs)

J F M A M J J A S O N D

It is clear how a journalist, researcher or author must ultimately choose one type of graph. But the question here is whether or not he/she is trying to make "his/her point" by choosing one type versus the other, rather than simply communicate some findings.

Please note that the bears, in our example, are shameless, and remain such in both instances, for they truly love honey!

Graphs were not used in this book. We were just too worried we wouldn't use the correct ones.

The Book Making Process

Research

We **researched** the name and address of every business and outdoor professional **in the United States and** in all the **provinces of Canada** (see list in the Appendix). Some states do not require guides and outfitters or businesses providing outdoor services to be registered, and in these instances the information must be obtained from many different sources [Outfitter's Associations, Marine Fisheries, Dept. of Tourism, Dept. of Environmental Conservation, Dept. of Natural Resources, Dept. of Fish and Game, US Coast Guard, Chamber of Commerce, etc.].

In the end the database on which we based this series of Top Rated™ Guides amounted to more than 23,000 names of Outfitters, Guides, Ranches, Captains etc. Our research continues and this number is increasing every day. The Appendix in the back of this book is only a partial list and refers specifically to Top Rated Paddling Adventures.

Participation

We **invited** businesses and outdoor professionals, with a letter and a brochure explaining the Top Rated concept, to join our endeavor by simply sending us a **complete** list of their clients of the past two years. With the "Confidentiality Statement" we reassured them that the list was going to be kept **absolutely confidential** and to be *used one time only* for the specific purpose of evaluating their operation. Then it would be destroyed.

We truly oppose this "black market" of names so abused by the mail marketing business. If you are ever contacted by Top Rated you may rest assured that your name, referred to us by your outdoor professional, will never be sold, traded or otherwise used a second time by us for marketing purposes.

Questionnaires

We then **sent a questionnaire** to **every single client on each list** (to a maximum of 300 randomly picked for those who submitted large lists with priority given to overnight or multiple day trips), asking them to rate the

services, the **knowledge** and **performance** of the business or outdoor professional by completing our comprehensive questionnaire (see pages 202-203). The businesses and outdoor professionals found in these pages may or may not be the ones who invest large sums of money to advertise in magazines, or to participate at the annual conventions of different clubs and foundations. However, they are clearly the ones, according to our survey, that put customer satisfaction and true dedication to their clients first and foremost.

Data Elaboration

A **numerical value was assigned to each question**. All the **scores were computed**. Both the **average** and the **median** were calculated and considered for eligibility. Please note that the total score was computed as a percentile value.

This allows some flexibility where one question was left unanswered or was answered with an N/A. Furthermore, we decided not to consider the high and the low score to ensure a more evenly distributed representation and to reduce the influence which an extreme judgement could have either way (especially with the small sample sizes).

We also set a **minimum number of questionnaires** which needed to be answered to allow a business or an outdoor professional to qualify. Such number was set as a function of the total number of clients in the list: the smaller the list of clients, the higher was the percentage of responses needed for qualification.

In some cases the outdoor professional's average score came within 1 point of the A- cutoff mark. In these instances, we considered both the median and the average were considered as well as the guests' comments and the total number of times that this particular business was recommended by the clients by answering with a 'yes' to questions 19 and 20.

Sharing the results

Top Rated™ Guides will share the results of this survey with the businesses and the outdoor professionals. This will be done at no cost to them whether or not they qualify for publication. All questionnaires received will, in fact, be returned along with a summary result to the business, keeping the confidentiality of the client's name when this was requested. This will prove an invaluable tool to help improve those areas that have received some criticisms.

The intention of this series of books is to research the opinions and the comments of outdoor enthusiasts, and to share the results of our research with the public and other key groups.

One outfitter wrote us about our Top Rated™ Guides series, "I feel your idea is an exciting and unique concept. Hopefully our past clientele will rate us with enough points to 'earn' a spot in your publication. If not, could we please get a copy of our points/questionnaires to see where we need to improve. Sincerely…"

This outfitter failed to qualify by just a few points, but such willingness to improve leaves us no doubt that his/her name will be one of those featured in our second edition. In the end it was not easy to exclude some of them from publication, but we are certain that, with the feedback provided by this survey, they will be able to improve those areas that need extra attention.

We made a real effort to keep a position of absolute impartiality in this process and, in this respect, we would like to repeat that the outdoor professionals have not paid, nor will they pay, one single penny to Top Rated™ Guides or the Editor to be included in this book.

The research continues.

Top Rated
Icon Legend

General Services and Accommodations

INFANT CARE

TODDLER PROGRAM

KIDS PROGRAMS

BABY SITTING

FAMILY

SENIOR CITIZEN

HANDICAP

ARCHEOLOGICAL SITES

FULL BOARD

GOURMET MEALS

HOT SPRINGS

General Services and Accommodations

Locations

General Services

Season(s) of operation

Activities

CATCH & RELEASE

FLY FISHING

SPIN CASTING

WHITEWATER FISHING

SEA KAYAKING

WHITEWATER TRIPS

SWIMMING

SCUBA DIVING

WAGON RIDES

CRABBING

FLY TYING SCHOOL

FLY FISHING SCHOOL

RAFTING /KAYAK SCHOOL

Activities

WILDLIFE VIEWING

WHALE WATCHING

BIRD WATCHING

HORSEBACK

HORSE PACK TRIPS

HIKING / TREKKING

CROSS COUNTRY

SNOWSHOEING

LLAMA PACK TRIPS

MOUNTAIN BIKING

CLAY SHOOTING

BIG GAME HUNTING

BIRD HUNTING

Boat Types and Transportation

CATARAFT

CANOE

McKENZIE / DORY

INFLATABLE KAYAK

RAFT

SEA KAYAKING

KAYAK

JET BOAT

FLOAT AIRPLANE

4X4 VEHICLE

River Classes of Difficulty

Top Rated
Guides and Outfitters

Alaska

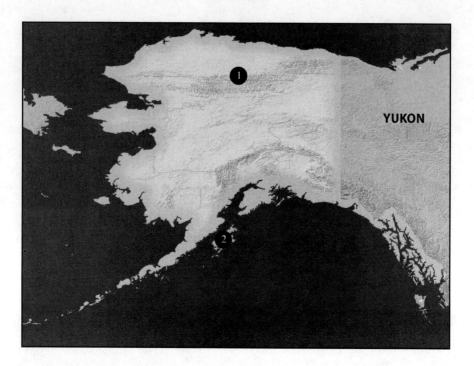

Outdoor Professionals

1 Alaska Fish and Trails Unlimited
2 Spirit of Alaska Wilderness Adventures

License and Report Requirements

• State requires licensing of Outdoor Professionals.

• State requires a "Hunt Record" for big game.

• Saltwater Charter Vessels Logbook Program - Charter Vessel guided trips are required to submit pages of logbook on a weekly basis.

• Charter Vessels are required to be licensed with the Commercial Fisheries Entry Commission at Juneau, phone: (907) 789-6150.

Useful information for the state of

Alaska

State and Federal Agencies

Alaska Dept. of Fish & Game
PO Box 25526
Juneau, AK 99802-5526
phone: (907) 465-4180 Fish
(907) 465-4190 Game

Alaska Region Forest Service
709 West 9th Street
Box 21628
Juneau, AK 99802-1628
phone: (907) 586-8863
TTY: (907) 586-7816
www.fs.fed.us/r10

Chugach National Forest
3301 C Street, Ste. 300
Anchorage, AK 99503-3998
phone: (907) 271-2500
TTY: (907) 271-2332

Tongass National Forest:
Sitka Office
204 Siginaka Way
Sitka, AK 99835
phone: (907) 747-6671
TTY: (907) 747-4535
fax: (907) 747-4331

Tongas National Forest:
Federal Building
Ketchikan, AK 99901-6591
phone: (907) 228-6202
fax: (907) 228-6215

Bureau of Land Management
Alaska State Office
222 W. 7th Avenue, #13
Anchorage, AK 99513-7599
phone: (907) 271-5960
or (907) 271-plus extension
fax: (907) 271-4596
http://www.ak.blm.gov

Office Hours: 8:00 a.m. - 3:45 p.m.

National Parks

Denali National Park & Preserve
phone: (907) 683-2294

Gates of the Arctic National Park
phone: (907) 456-0281

Glacier Bay National Park
phone: (907) 697-2230

Katmai National Park
phone: (907) 246-3305

Kenai Fjords National Park
phone: (907) 224-3175

Kobuk Valley National Park
phone: (907) 442-3890

Lake Clark National Park
phone: (907) 271-3751

Wrangell-St. Elias National Park
phone: (907) 822-5234

Yukon-Charley Rivers National Park
phone: (907) 456-0593

Associations, Publications, etc.

American Fisheries Society
2720 Set Net Ct.
Kenai, AK 99611
phone: (907) 260-2909
fax: (907) 262-7646

Trout Unlimited Alaska Council
PO Box 3055
Soldotna, AK 99669
phone: (907) 262-9494

Federation of Fly Fishers
http://www.fedflyfishers.org

Alaska Fish and Trails Unlimited

Jerald D. Stansel

1177 Shypoke Dr. • Fairbanks, AK 99709
PO Box 26045, Bettles Field, AK 99726
phone: (907) 479-7630 • www.ptialaska.net/~aktrails

Alaska Fish and Trails Unlimited is owned by guide and bush pilot Jerry Stansel, who has been operating and guiding in the Brooks Range Gates of the Arctic for 25 years.

His tours specialize in guided and unguided fly-in fishing, rafting, backpacking and photography trips.

Species of fish include arctic char, sheefish, lake trout, arctic grayling, whitefish, northern pike and salmon.

So come, breathe Alaska's crisp, clean air. Drink its pure, fresh water. Fly across the Arctic Circle and Arctic Divide. Fish for a variety of species, either around Fairbanks or in the Arctic.

"Caught and Released over 100 lake trout, all but one over 10 lbs. Caught one pike over 48 inches!!"
  Keith Smith

SEASONS OF OPERATION

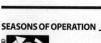

BOAT TYPES

ACTIVITIES

LOCATIONS & SERVICES

Alaska Fish &
Trails Unlimited

Spirit of Alaska Wilderness Adventures

Steel Davis, owner/operator & Jeannie Dennis, reservations/information
P.O. Box 4391 • Kodiak, AK 99615
phone: (907) 487-2379 (day) • (907) 486-3564 (message)
email: spirit-of-alaska@usa.net

Spirit of Alaska offers a wide variety of activities, from kayaking to some of the finest fishing and wildlife viewing in the world. We are located in Uyak Bay on Amook Island.

Our facility is designed for the do-it-yourselfer. A knowledgeable salt and freshwater fishing guide, who is also a certified sea captain and kayak instructor is at your disposal.

A private, warm, cozy cabin is provided with running water, propane lights, refrigerator, stove and oven. An 8-by-12-foot sauna is attached. An outside privy is used.

Sea kayaking is one of the fastest growing sports in the world. Our location provides calm waters and some of the finest wildlife viewing to be found anywhere.

"A truly wilderness experience!"
Norville R. Broadbent

SEASONS OF OPERATION

BOAT TYPES

ACTIVITIES

LOCATIONS & SERVICES

Spirit of Alaska Wilderness Adventures

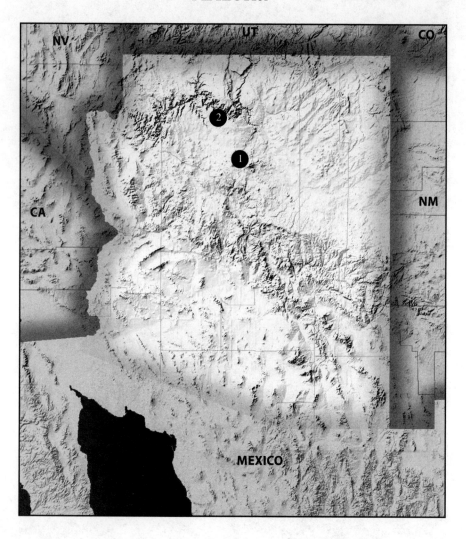

Outdoor Professionals

1 Canyon R.E.O.
2 Grand Canyon Dories - O.A.R.S.

Arizona

State and Federal Agencies

Arizona Game & Fish Dept.
2221 West Greenway Rd.
Phoenix, AZ 85023
phone: (602) 942-3000
fax: (602) 789-3924

Forest Service
Southwestern Region
Federal Building
517 Gold Avenue SW
Albuquerque, NM 87102
phone: (505) 842-3300

Apache-Sitgreaves National Forests
phone: (520) 333-4301

Coconino National Forest
phone: (520) 527-3600

Coronado National Forest
phone: (520) 670-4552

Kaibab National Forest
phone: (520) 635-8200

Prescott National Forest
phone: (520) 771-4700

Tonto National Forest
phone: (602) 225-5200

Bureau of Land Management
Arizona State Office
222 North Central Avenue
P.O. Box 555
Phoenix, AZ 85004-2203
phone: (602) 417-9200
or (602) 417-plus ext.
fax: (602) 417-9556

Office Hours: 7:45 a.m. - 4:15 p.m.

National Parks

Grand Canyon National Park
phone: (520) 638-7888

Grand Canyon River Outfitters Association
PO Box 22189
Flagstaff, AZ 86002
phone: (520) 556-0669
fax: (520) 556-3155
Email: gcroa@gcroa.com
http://www.grcoa.com

Associations, Publications, etc.

Prescott Paddle America Club
PO Box 12098
Prescott, AZ 86304
phone: (520) 445-5480

License and Report Requirements

• State requires licensing of Outdoor Professionals.

• State requires an "End of Year Guides Report" for all outdoor guided activities.

• "Use permit" required for anyone using BLM, National Forest, Indian reservations, and National Parks for rafting, back packing, big game, fishing, etc. Guides required to file "End of Year Guides Report" for all activities on Federal Lands.

Canyon R.E.O.

Donnie Dove

P.O. Box 3493 • Flagstaff, AZ 86003-3493
phone: (800) 637-4604 • (520) 774-3377 • fax: (520) 774-3343
email: canyonreo@thecanyon.com • www.thecanyon.com/canyonreo

Break away from your world to experience the magnificence of the Chama River and Upper San Juan. Whether you seek a family vacation or the rush of a whitewater adventure, Canyon R.E.O. will introduce you to this magical wilderness experience.

We offer kayak, canoe, and raft instruction in special novice and intermediate courses.

Let us customize a trip for your group. The staff is skilled in all facets: oarsman, guide, chef, storyteller, naturalist, teacher and friend.

All ages from 7 to 80. No prior river or camping experience needed. If you have a special dietary/physical need, let us know. We facilitate trips for handicapped and special needs groups.

All river equipment, lifejackets, safety equipment, waterproof clothing storage, hearty and wholesome riverside meals are provided.

"...it was our first raft ride and we look forward to do it again"
John Barber

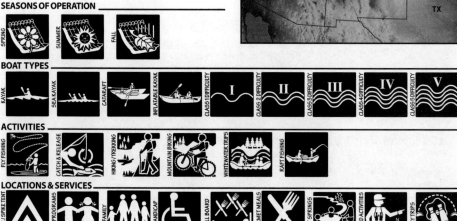

CANYON R.E.O.
RIVER EQUIPMENT OUTFITTERS

Grand Canyon Dories - O.A.R.S.

George Wendt

P.O. Box 67 • *Angels Camp, CA 95222*
phone: (800) 346-6277 • (209) 736-0811 • *fax: (209) 736-2902* • (209) 736-6776 *24 hour information line*
email: *reservations@oars.com* • *www.oars.com/gcdories*

Martin Litton, the famous river-runner, writer, Sunset magazine editor, and environmental crusader, founded Grand Canyon Dories. He built a company that believed in hiring well-educated guides who thoroughly loved the rivers and their history, and never shied away from the heat of adventure. O.A.R.S. (Outdoor Adventure River Specialists) and Grand Canyon Dories proudly carry on the tradition of Litton's original company.

We offer these beautiful, legendary boats on a wide variety of river trips (ranging from 3-19 days) throughout Utah, Idaho, early season trips in Oregon, and of course, the Grand Canyon.

Seasoned river-runners will tell you that the dory is the only way to go. We are also the only company in the world to offer whitewater dory instruction.

"I went because I wanted the "ultimate" whitewater experience. I came away with much, much more! I would go with Grand Canyon Dories again in a heartbeat!"
Patricia Poirier

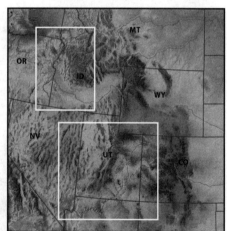

SEASONS OF OPERATION

SPRING · SUMMER · FALL

BOAT TYPES

McKENZIE / DORY · RAFT · CLASS 3 DIFFICULTY III · CLASS 4 DIFFICULTY IV · CLASS 5 DIFFICULTY V

ACTIVITIES

FLY FISHING · CATCH & RELEASE · WHITEWATER TRIPS · HOT SPRINGS · ARCHEOLOGICAL SITES

LOCATIONS & SERVICES

LODGE · DOME / SPIKE TENT · KIDS PROGRAMS · FAMILY · HANDICAP · FULL BOARD · GOURMET MEALS · GUIDED ACTIVITIES · DAY TRIPS

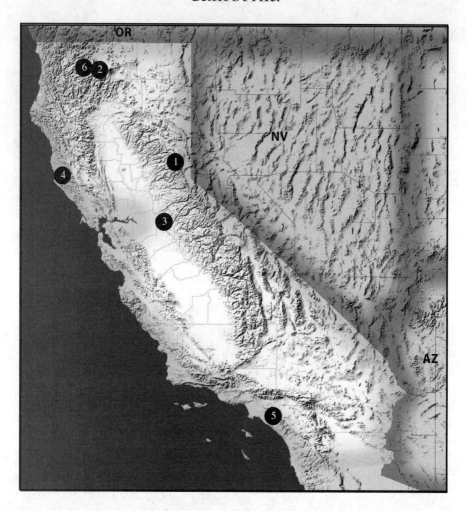

Outdoor Professionals

1. I.R.I.E Rafting Company
2. Living Waters Recreation
3. O.A.R.S. - Outdoor Adventure River Specialists
4. River Travel Center
5. Southwind Kayak Center, Inc.
6. Turtle River Rafting Company

California

State and Federal Agencies

California Fish & Game Commission
License & Revenue Branch
3211 "S" Street
Sacramento, CA 95816
phone: (916) 227-2245
fax: (916) 227-2261
http://www.dfg.ca.gov

Pacific Southwest
Forest Service Region
630 Sansome St.
San Francisco, CA 94111
phone: (415) 705-2874
TTY: (415) 705-1098

Bureau of Land Management
California State Office
2800 Cottage Way
Sacramento, CA 95825
fax: (916) 978-4657
http://www.ca.blm.gov

Office Hours: 8:30 - 4:30 pm (PST)

National Parks

Lassen Volcanic National Park
phone: (530) 595-4444

Redwood National Park
phone: (707) 464-6101

Sequoia & Kings Canyon Natl. Parks
phone: (209) 565-3341

Yosemite National Park
phone: (209) 372-0200

Channel Islands National Park
phone: (805) 658-5700

Associations, Publications, etc.

California Trout, Inc.
870 Market St. #859
San Francisco, CA 94102
phone: (415) 392-8887
http://www.caltrout.org

Trout Unlimited, California Chapter
1024 C. Los Gamos
San Rafael, CA 94903-2517
phone: (415) 472-5837
http://cwo.com/~trout/index.html

Federation of Fly Fishers
http://www.fedflyfishers.org
Bass Chapter Federation
751 Melva Ave.
Oakdale, CA 95361
phone: (209) 541-3673
or (209) 847-3272

California Outdoors
PO Box 401
Coloma, CA 95613
phone: (800) 552-3625
http://www.caloutdoor.org

License and Report Requirements
• State requires licensing of Outdoor Professionals.
• State requires the filing of a "Monthly Guide Log" for all outdoor professionals, including river outfitters.
• River Outfitters need a "Use Permit", required for BLM, National Forest, Indian reservations, and National Parks.
• Boat and Waterways Dept. requires license for all motorized craft, and raft or floating device if carrying more than 3 persons.

I.R.I.E Rafting Company

Amy and Frank E. Wohlfahrt

P.O. Box 3150 • Olympic Valley, CA 96146
phone: (888) 969-IRIE • (916) 587-1184

We invite you to experience a distinct I.R.I.E. River Expedition.

Whether you desire a leisurely float downstream with friends and family or a white-knuckle test of teamwork, let I.R.I.E. indulge your senses while sharing the beauty and excitement of wild river canyons.

I.R.I.E. Rafting Company implements low-impact environmental ethics, demonstrating how everyday habits help preserve our scenic areas. Interpretive education about geographic history, flora and fauna enriches even the most exciting rivers.

Escape with I.R.I.E. Rafting Company for a regenerating outdoors experience.

See you on the river!

"It was the description of the river and surrounding area that made our outing enjoyable....Doug was a great guide!"
Russ Noel

SEASONS OF OPERATION

SPRING • SUMMER • FALL

BOAT TYPES

CATARAFT • RAFT • INFLATABLE KAYAK • CLASS 2 DIFFICULTY **II** • CLASS 6.5 DIFFICULTY **III** • CLASS 6.4 DIFFICULTY **IV** • CLASS 6.5 DIFFICULTY **V**

ACTIVITIES

FLY FISHING • CATCH & RELEASE • WHITEWATER TRIPS • HOT SPRINGS • ARCHEOLOGICAL SITES • HORSE PACK TRIPS • HIKING / TREKKING

LOCATIONS & SERVICES

DOME / SPIKE TENT • KIDS PROGRAMS • FAMILY • HANDICAP • FULL BOARD • GOURMET MEALS • WOMEN ONLY TRIPS • GUIDED ACTIVITIES • DAY TRIPS

Living Waters Recreation

Tom Harris

P.O. Box 1192 • Mt. Shasta, CA 96067-1192
phone: (800) 994 RAFT (7238) • fax: (530) 926-5446
email: livingwaters@telis.org • www.livingwatersrec.com

We invite your family and friends to share our love and enthusiasm for rafting Northern California's unique and uncrowded rivers where we put your safety first.

From mild to wild, we have a rafting adventure tailor-made for you. Half-day, full-day, and two- and three-day trips available. Full-day trips enjoy a deluxe buffet deli lunch. Two- and three-day trips also provide gourmet-cooked meals.

All our guides are professionals trained in swiftwater rescue skills, first aid, and CPR. They are dedicated to making your trip the safest and best ever.

All safety equipment is provided, with free use of wetsuits and splash jackets. Family and group discounts. Free trips (call for details).

Call for brochure, or visit our website.

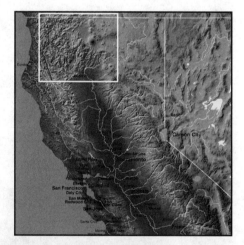

"Just a very fine trip" Bob Osborn

SEASONS OF OPERATION

BOAT TYPES

ACTIVITIES

LOCATIONS & SERVICES

O.A.R.S.-Outdoor Adventure River Specialists

George Wendt

P.O. Box 67 • Angels Camp, CA 95222
phone: (800) 346-6277 • (209) 736-4677 • email: reservations@oars.com • www.oars.com
fax: (209) 736-2902 • (209) 736-6776 - 24 hour information line

O.A.R.S. (Outdoor Adventure River Specialists) was the first small raft, oar-powered outfitter in the Grand Canyon.

In 1970, they forever changed the face of river travel. By challenging the myth that adventure had to be ridiculously uncomfortable, they built a reputation for leading guests on ultra-comfortable expeditions that are accessible to everyone — no matter who you are, you can experience the joys of the backcountry.

O.A.R.S. offers wilderness vacations and whitewater adventures from 1-19 days throughout the West and internationally. Come along for the journey and experience the wonders of places such as California's Tuolumne River, Oregon's Rogue, Idaho's Middle Fork Salmon, Utah's Cataract Canyon and, of course, the Colorado through the Grand Canyon.

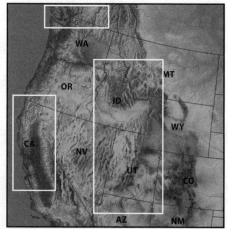

"The OARS trip was the best adventure we ever had! We are definitely planning to go on another OARS trip!" Joan Tommaney

SEASONS OF OPERATION

SPRING | SUMMER | FALL

BOAT TYPES

RAFT | INFLATABLE KAYAK | CLASS 1 DIFFICULTY I | CLASS 2 DIFFICULTY II | CLASS 3 DIFFICULTY III | CLASS 4 DIFFICULTY IV | CLASS 5 DIFFICULTY V

ACTIVITIES

FLY FISHING | CATCH & RELEASE | HIKING/TREKKING | WHITEWATER TRIPS | ARCHEOLOGICAL SITES | HOT SPRINGS | RAFTING/KAYAK SCHOOL

LOCATIONS & SERVICES

BLUERIBBONSTREAM | LODGE | DOME / SPIKE TENT | KIDS PROGRAMS | FAMILY | FULL BOARD | GOURMET MEALS | GUIDED ACTIVITIES | DAY TRIPS

58

OARS

*Outdoor Adventure
River Specialists*

River Travel Center

Annie Nelson, Raven Earlygrow, Prudence Parker

15 Riverside Drive • P.O. Box 6 • Point Arena, CA 95468
phone: (800) 882-7238 • (707) 882-2258 • fax: (707) 882-2638
email: annien@rivers.com

We specialize in arranging 2 to 21 day trips to the most beautiful and spectacular places on our planet. Our 16 Grand Canyon companies give us the widest range of options for Colorado River trips: oar or paddle-powered or motorized rafts, Las Vegas or Flagstaff departures, individuals or groups. Or, head for the wilderness of Idaho's Snake River through Hells Canyon, or the mighty Salmon. Try the West Coast's best family rafting on Oregon's Rogue River or the Green or Yampa in Utah.

Head south in the wintertime to warm and lovely Central America, where we can arrange delightful sea-kayaking or rafting excursions in Belize and Costa Rica. If you'd like to go farther, there are rivers to run in New Zealand, Nepal, Zambia, and the stunning wilds of Alaska. Wherever you'd like to go, we can help you get there.

"The canyon was magnificent and the people guiding my trip were great, knowledgeable, competent, pleasant and accommodating!" Ellen Fleishman

SEASONS OF OPERATION

River Travel Center

Southwind Kayak Center, Inc.

Doug Schwartz and Joanne Turner

17855 Sky Park Circle #A • Irvine, CA 92614
phone: (800) SOUTHWIND (800-768-8494) • (949) 261-0200 • http://www.southwindkayaks.com
email: info@southwindkayaks.com • doug@southwindkayaks.com • joanne@southwindkayaks.com

Our trips let you explore, relax, exercise and just have fun. Trips offer many opportunities to understand our natural environment - interpretation of animal, plant and bird life is part of all Southwind trips. We make every effort to ensure that our presence in an environment does not disturb the local wildlife, causing them to change their behavior. Because we want you and others visiting each area to feel it is being explored for the first time, low-impact camping is the key to the "Southwind style". Trips are also an opportunity for you to continue developing your kayak skills. Since Southwind guides are also professional kayak instructors, we can work with you on any aspect of your skills you desire, from the basic touring stroke to surf landing and advanced rock garden techniques.

Whether you go for a day out or venture far away, you'll find everything you need here at Southwind.

"These guides and staff are the best reason to come back (in addition to) the trip variety. I often recommend this great company to others!" Amy Senstad, Lighting Designer, Walt Disney Imagineering

SEASONS OF OPERATION

BOAT TYPES

ACTIVITIES

LOCATIONS & SERVICES

Turtle River Rafting Company

Rick Demarest

P.O. Box 313 • Mount Shasta, CA 96067
phone: (800) 726-3223 • (530) 926-3223 • fax: (530) 926-3443
email: raft@turtleriver.com • www.turtleriver.com

Welcome to Turtle River. Since 1976 we have been guiding whitewater rafting trips on the rivers of northern California and southern Oregon. Our trips are from 1 to 5 days. They include: mild whitewater and float trips where families can take children as young as four; more adventurous Class 3 wilderness trips; and wild-water Class 4 & 5. Our season begins in April with spring snow melt feeding the Salmon, Scott, Rogue, Upper Sacramento, and Owyhee rivers. By mid-June the days...and the water...begin to warm and summer finds us on the Trinity, Lower, Middle, and Upper Klamath. In September we add the Rogue River to our summer schedule.

We invite you to travel with us on a river adventure and share our love of whitewater, wilderness, and friendship...and we wish you a safe journey through the year...wherever the river takes you.

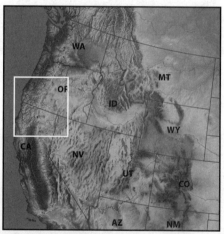

"We saw fabulous wildlife, few humans; the weather was awesome; our guide was fun, knowledgeable and a great chef...we hit the right combination!" Ben Davoren, Larkspur, CA

SEASONS OF OPERATION

SPRING SUMMER FALL

BOAT TYPES

RAFT INFLATABLE KAYAK CATARAFT CLASS 1 DIFFICULTY — I CLASS 2 DIFFICULTY — II CLASS 3 DIFFICULTY — III CLASS 4 DIFFICULTY — IV CLASS 5 DIFFICULTY — V

ACTIVITIES

FLY FISHING CATCH & RELEASE HIKING/TREKKING WHITEWATER TRIPS RAFTING/KAYAK SCHOOL

LOCATIONS & SERVICES

LARGE RIVER KIDS PROGRAMS FAMILY HANDICAP GOURMET MEALS DOME/SPIKE TENT GUIDED ACTIVITIES DAY TRIPS

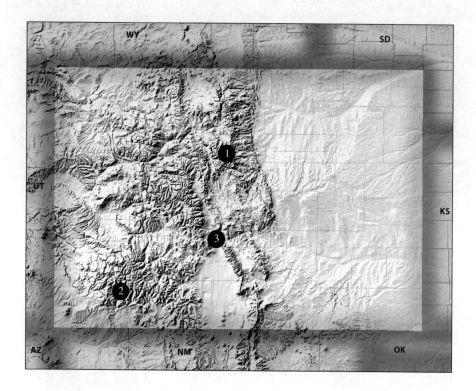

Outdoor Professionals

1. Bill Dvorak's Kayak & Rafting Expeditions
2. Mild To Wild Rafting
3. Whitewater Voyageurs

License and Report Requirements

• State requires licensing of Outdoor Professionals.

• State requires an "Inter-Office Copy of Contract with Client" be submitted each time a client goes with an Outfitter. Colorado Agencies of Outfitters Registry sends this copy to client to fill out and return to their agency.

• Colorado State Forest Service requires a "Use Permit" for all guided activities on federal land.

Useful information for the state of
Colorado

State and Federal Agencies

Colorado Agencies of Outfitters Registry
1560 Broadway, Suite 1340
Denver, CO 80202
phone: (303) 894-7778

Colorado Dept. of Natural Resources
1313 Sherman, Room 718
Denver, CO 80203
phone: (303) 866-3311

Forest Service
Rocky Mountain Region
740 Simms Street
PO Box 25127
Lakewood, CO 80225
phone: (303) 275-5350
TTY: (303) 275-5367

Arapaho-Roosevelt National Forests
Pawnee National Grassland
phone: (970) 498-2770

Grand Mesa-Umcompahgre
Gunnison National Forests
phone: (970) 874-7641

Pike-San Isabel National Forests
Commanche & Cimarron National
Grasslands
phone: (719) 545-8737

San Juan-Rio Grande National Forest
phone: (719) 852-5941

White River National Forest
phone: (970) 945-2521

Bureau of Land Management
Colorado State Office
2850 Youngfield St.
Lakewood, CO 80215-7093
phone: (303) 239-3600
fax: (303) 239-3933
Tdd: (303) 239-3635
Email: msowa@co.blm.gov
Office Hours: 7:45 a.m. - 4:15 p.m.

National Parks

Mesa Verde National Park, CO 81330
phone: (303) 529-4465

Rocky Mountain National Park
phone: (303) 586-2371

Associations, Publications, etc.

Colorado Whitewater Association
2 Silver Cloud
Boulder, CO 80302
phone: (303) 447-0068
fax: (303) 776-4068

Colorado Whitewater Association
PO Box 4315
Englewood, CO 80155-4315
phone: (303) 430-4853

Paddler Magazine
PO Box 775450
Steamboat Springs, CO 80477
phone/fax: (303) 879-1450

Bill Dvořák's Kayak & Rafting Expeditions

Bill and Jaci Dvořak

17921 U.S. Hwy. 285 • Nathrop, CO 81236
reservations: (800) 824-3795 • office: (719) 539-6851 • fax: (719) 539-3378
email: dvorakex@amigo.net • http://www.dvorakexpeditions.com

Bill and I invite you to join us for the adventure of a lifetime. We have been guiding river and wilderness trips since 1969 and have one of the most experienced and best trained staffs in the industry.

We have successfully combined high adventure with professionalism for more than 25 years. We've watched our children grow up on the river, we've seen the staff and guests respond to being on the river, and we know there is a powerful moving effect a river has on us all.

Everyone deserves a chance to experience such river magic. Our trips make it easy for you to enjoy the best of whitewater beauty and adventure.

Choose the trip that best suits you, or ask for a customized group trip.

Make this season your year for the adventure of a lifetime!

"Everything they do is first class and when you leave, you feel like you are leaving family." Walter L. Fuller

SEASONS OF OPERATION

SPRING · SUMMER · FALL

BOAT TYPES

RAFT · INFLATABLE KAYAK · CATARAFT · SEA KAYAK · CLASS 1 DIFFICULTY · I · CLASS 2 DIFFICULTY · II · CLASS 3 DIFFICULTY · III · CLASS 4 DIFFICULTY · IV · CLASS 5 DIFFICULTY · V

ACTIVITIES

SEA KAYAKING · FLY FISHING · CATCH & RELEASE · HIKING/TREKKING · BIG GAME HUNTING · WHITEWATER TRIPS · ARCHEOLOGICAL SITES · RAFTING/KAYAK SCHOOL

LOCATIONS & SERVICES

LARGE RIVER · KIDS PROGRAMS · FAMILY · HANDICAP · FULL BOARD · GOURMET MEALS · DOME/SPIKE TENT · GUIDED ACTIVITIES · DAY TRIPS

Mild to Wild Rafting

Alex and Molly Mickel

11 Rio Vista Circle • Durango, CO 81302
phone: (800) 567-6745 • (970) 247-4789 • fax: (970) 382-0545
email: mildwild@rmii.com • http://www.mild2wildrafting.com

Mild to Wild Rafting has a river trip for all ages (3-93) and all adventure levels in beautiful Southwest Colorado.

Enjoy an exciting family trip (two hours to four days) on the Animas, San Juan, or Dolores rivers. The more adventurouse ones can also experience an intermediate trip on the Upper Dolores or Upper Piedra rivers (nine full days).

For the ultimate high adventure try the big drops of the Piedra River (one to two days), or go for an adrenaline rush on one of the toughest commercially-run rivers in the USA — the Upper Animas River (one to three days).

We guarantee your absolute delight with our services and guides or the trip is on us. Call for a free color brochure.

"It was an outstanding day! Never had so much fun on an outing as we did... a special plus was their ability to accommodate passengers that were in wheelchairs!" Bob Bahl

SEASONS OF OPERATION

BOAT TYPES

ACTIVITIES

LOCATIONS & SERVICES

Mild to Wild
R A F T I N G

Whitewater Voyageurs

John Sells

P.O. Box 346 • Poncha Springs, CO 81242
phone: (800) 255-2585 • (719) 539-7618 • fax: (719) 539-7610
email: john@mtnspts.com • www.mtnspts.com

Whitewater Voyageurs has successfully operated on the Arkansas River for more than 20 years. We are proud to offer the most highly-trained and experienced staff in the industry.

We respect our guests' needs and do everything within reason to ensure their satisfaction. With our motivated and knowledgeable team, we maintain our commitment to excellence and continually offer higher quality, more innovative adventure packages. In a world of constant environmental abuse, we vow to take every action possible to uphold the pristine majesty of the Rocky Mountain area we inhabit.

Whitewater Voyageurs is a member of the Colorado River Outfitters Association, Arkansas River Outfitters Association, America Outdoors, and licensed through the state of Colorado as a commercial river outfitter.

"Moot's low-key style was a perfect balance for an exciting and sometimes heartstopping experience...what a blast!"
Lisa Stockton

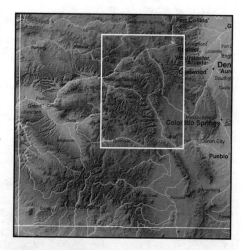

SEASONS OF OPERATION

BOAT TYPES

ACTIVITIES

LOCATIONS & SERVICES

Whitewater Voyageurs

Idaho

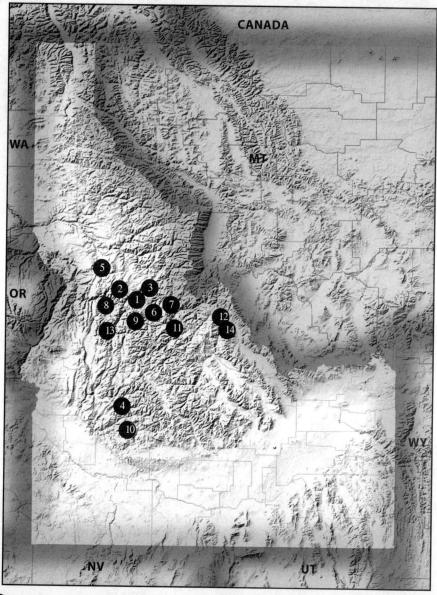

1. Aggipah River Trips
2. Canyon Cats
3. Clearwater River Co.
4. Headwaters River Co.
5. Idaho Afloat
6. Middle Fork River Tours
7. Moser's Idaho Adventures
8. Northwest Voyageurs
9. Rawhide Outfitters
10. Rocky Mountain River Tours
11. Silver Cloud Expeditions
12. Solitude River Trips
13. Wapiti River Guides
14. Warren River Expeditions

Idaho

State and Federal Agencies

Idaho Fish & Game Dept.
600 SouthWalnut
Boise, ID 83707
phone: (208) 334-3700
fax: (208) 334-2114

Outfitter & Guides Licensing Board
1365 N. Orchard, Room 172
Boise, ID 83706
phone: (208) 327-7380
fax: (208) 327-7382

Forest Service
Northern Region
Federal Bldg.
PO Box 7669
Missoula, MT 59807-7669
phone: (406) 329-3616
TTY: (406) 329-3510

Clearwater National Forest
phone: (208) 476-4541

Idaho Panhandle, Coeur d'Alene, Kaniksu,
St. Joe National Forests
phone / TTY: (208) 765-7223

Nez Perce National Forest
phone: (208) 983-1950

Bureau of Land Management
Idaho State Office
1387 S.VinnellWay
Boise, ID 83709-1657
phone: (208) 373-3896
or (208) 373-plus extension
fax: (208) 373-3899
Office Hours 7:45 a.m. - 4:15 p.m.

Associations, Publications, etc.

Trout Unlimited Idaho Council
212 N. Fourth Street #145
Sandpoint, ID 83864-9466
phone: (208) 263-4433
fax: (208) 265-2996

American Fisheries Society
Edward D. Koch
3765 La MesitaWay
Boise, ID 83072
phone: (208) 378-5293
Email: ted_koch@mail.fws.gov

Federation of Fly Fishers
http://www.fedflyfishers.org

Idaho Bass Chapter Federation
President: Allan Chandler
9906W. Deep Canyon Drive
Star, ID 83669
phone: (208) 859-5433 (day)
Email: chandlr@micron.net

Idaho Outfitters & Guides Association
PO Box 95
Boise, ID 83701
phone: (208) 342-1438
fax: (208) 338-7830
Email: info@ioga.org • http://www.ioga.org

License and Report Requirements

• State requires licensing of Outdoor Professionals.
• State requires that every Outfitter be it bird, fish, big game, river rafting, trail riding or packing file a "Use Report" annually.
• Bureau of Land Management requires Special Use Permit for commercial guiding on BLM property.
• Currently, no requirements for Guest/Dude Ranches.

Aggipah River Trips

Bill and Peggy Bernt
Box 425 • Salmon, ID 83467
phone: (208) 756-4167 • email: bill@aggipah.com

In addition to conventional multi-day summer trips on all three roadless sections of the Salmon, the Middle Fork, the Main and the Lower Salmon, specialty trips include fishing trips for trout and steelhead; combination horseback/float trips; trips with nights at lodges along the river instead of camping; off-season trips with maximum solitude, wildlife, and wildflowers; private, charter trips; a watercolor painting workshop; and a local history trip.

I have spent 30 years learning the Salmon River country, floating each summer, spending the off-season doing an M.S. in wildlife biology and agency work with game counts and distribution, riding the high-country trails, digging into the history of the area, and, especially, living along the Salmon. Our trips are first class, with mature, local boatmen, dutch-oven and open-fire cooking, regional dinner wines, ice and fresh foods throughout the trip, tables and chairs, and top-quality equipment.

"The quality of the Aggipah River Trips organization was equal to the beauty of the Middle Fork of the Salmon River. Bill Bernt & his crew exceeded what anyone could expect." Rem Kohrt, Whitefish, MT

SEASONS OF OPERATION

BOAT TYPES

ACTIVITIES

LOCATIONS & SERVICES

Canyon Cats

Gail Ater, Owner and Roy Akins, Manager

215 N. Main Street • PO Box 11 • Riggins, ID 83549
phone: (888) 628-3772 • (Riggins) (208) 628-3772 • (Gooding) (208) 934-4810
email: info@canyoncats.com • www.canyoncats.com

We specialize in customizing river excursions on the majestic Salmon River of Idaho for families, groups, and individuals ranging in length from a half-day to five days. Canyon Cats operates exclusively with the use of catarafts: two (2) pontoons supported with rigid frames, which are faster, more maneuverable, and safer than conventional rafts. We practice low impact camping and we try to leave only footprints when passing through the river corridor.

The natural world is for everyone to enjoy. Canyon Cats' guides are full time professionals who are serious about what they do. When not guiding they are actively involved in learning and perfecting new skills or learning new facts about the local geology and Native American history, including the Lewis and Clark expedition. Also, the flora and fauna in this unique area are diverse and commonly seen and discussed. We believe that the Salmon River is a vital source of life for the plants, animals and humans that live within its canyons. Come and share the magic.

"Mike knows this river well, I trust his judgement at all times. Thanks Canyon Cats for this unforgettable whitewater adventure. You are the best!" Jason M. Edwards

SEASONS OF OPERATION

BOAT TYPES

ACTIVITIES

LOCATIONS & SERVICES

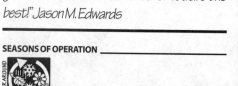

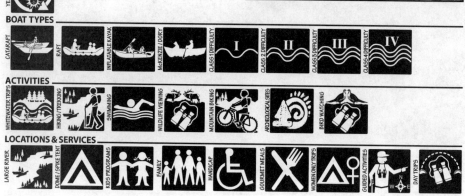

Clearwater River Company

Jim Cook

11330 Highway 12 • Orofino, ID 83544
phone: (208) 476-9199 • fax: (208) 476-9338
email: clrwtr@clearwatertrips.com • www.clearwatertrips.com

Our mission is to offer you and your family a safe, comfortable, unforgettable river experience. Relaxation, with a mix of history, adventure and excitement is what we seek in every trip. We specialize in historical, educational, and cultural trips of discovery, and drift-boat fishing trips. Catching glimpses of the local wildlife and recalling images of Clearwater Country's past: Chief Joseph, Lewis & Clark and the gold rush days.

As you step out of your river craft into our Native American Indian Encampment you will have the opportunity to experience, through hands-on activities, many of the skills that sustained not only the Lewis and Clark expedition but many cultures past and present for thousands of years. We also have the finest dining on the Clearwater! We invite families, groups, clubs, , and individuals of all ages to join us on this exciting journey.

"My kids still talk about Teepee camp where they learned the primitive skills of building a fire, grinding corn, making rope from Yucca leaves, and tracking animals in the wild. A magical world of what North American life once was." David Rassmussen

SEASONS OF OPERATION _____

BOAT TYPES _____

ACTIVITIES _____

LOCATIONS & SERVICES _____

Headwaters River Company

Julie Beppu and Betsy Bader

P. O. Box 1 • Banks, ID 83602
phone: (800) 800 RAFT (7238) • (208) 793-2348
email: rafting@micron.net • http://netnow.micron.net/~rafting/

The Payette rivers are the whitewater state's best-kept secret. With Headwaters you can explore the South Fork, North Fork or Main Payette.

The Payette River system contains a myriad of opportunities for whitewater experiences, from a scenic Class I float to an adrenaline pumping, white-knuckled Class IV ride. Choose from half-day, one-day, or multi-day trips.

It is our goal to provide each of our guests with the best river trip, from the guide and food to the whitewater. We have wonderful kayak instructors who have a penchant for teaching. The only prerequisite is an attitude for fun. Our guides average eight years guiding experience and are licensed by the state of Idaho. All full-time guides hold First Responder medical cards.

"An outstanding whitewater experience by a friendly, professional staff...A remarkable trip." Tom Lillie

SEASONS OF OPERATION

BOAT TYPES

ACTIVITIES

LOCATIONS & SERVICES

82

HEADWATERS
RIVER COMPANY

Idaho Afloat

Bruce Howard

P.O. Box 542 • Grangeville, ID 83530
phone: (800) 700-2414 • (208) 983-2414 • fax: (208) 983-9259
email: idafloat@camesnet.com • www.idafloat.com

Idaho Afloat provides deluxe whitewater rafting adventures on the Snake River through Hells Canyon and on the Lower Salmon River. Our trips offer families, first-time and experienced rafters a variety of multi-day soft adventure excitement.

The Snake River through Hells Canyon (rated Class IV) is the deepest canyon in North America and has the most powerful whitewater in the Northwest. You will run the rapids, see ancient pictographs, explore old homesteads, hike riverside trails, and have time to relax and enjoy the sounds of nature.

The Lower Salmon River Gorge (Class III) offers solitude, four spectacular canyons, and incredible white sandy beaches with clear and cool pools for swimming and daydreaming.

Join Idaho Afloat for a memory of a lifetime. Sit back and let it happen.

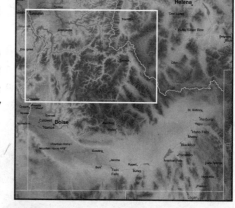

"We were treated like royalty and the only surprises we had turned out to be that this trip got better by the minute."
John & Lydia Hecker

SEASONS OF OPERATION

BOAT TYPES

ACTIVITIES

LOCATIONS & SERVICES

Middle Fork River Tours

Kurt and Gayle Selisch

P.O. Box 2222 • Hailey, ID 83333
phone: (800) 445-9738 • fax: (208) 788-7028
email: mfrt@sunvalley.net • www.middlefork.com

Idaho's Middle Fork of the Salmon is renowned as America's premier wilderness river. Please join us and float 105 miles through a pristine wilderness canyon that offers legendary whitewater, backcountry solitude, natural hot springs, abundant wildlife, and fabulous fishing. Experience this spectacular river in your choice of oar-raft, paddle-raft, inflatable kayak, or drift boat.

Middle Fork River Tours is an owner-operated outfitter that offers only the finest river vacation. By choice we have remained a small and specialized company that runs only the Middle Fork. Providing personalized service to each trip and every guest is a priority. From our quality equipment and outstanding staff, to the wine list accompanying our 5 star meals, we set our standards higher.

Please join us; we guarantee you a first class experience.

"Convivial spirits of the guides, incredible beauty of the Middle Fork of the Snake River, and gastronomical delights prepared daily make it extraordinary. What a refined pleasure!" Greg & Wita Wojtkowski, Boise, ID

SEASONS OF OPERATION

SPRING | SUMMER | FALL

BOAT TYPES

RAFT | INFLATABLE KAYAK | McKENZIE/DORY | CLASS 1 DIFFICULTY | CLASS 2 DIFFICULTY | CLASS 3 DIFFICULTY | CLASS 4 DIFFICULTY | CLASS 5 DIFFICULTY | RAFTING/KAYAK SCHOOL

ACTIVITIES

WHITEWATER TRIPS | FLY FISHING | HIKING/TREKKING | WILDLIFE VIEWING | ARCHEOLOGICAL SITES | HOT SPRINGS | MOUNTAIN BIKING | BIRD HUNTING | HORSE PACK TRIPS

LOCATIONS & SERVICES

LARGE RIVER | DOME/SPIKE TENT | KIDS PROGRAMS | FAMILY | HANDICAP | GOURMET MEALS | WOMEN ONLY TRIPS | GUIDED ACTIVITIES | OVERNIGHT TRIPS

Middle Fork River Tours

Moser's Idaho Adventures

Gary and Paula Moser

P.O. Box 834 • Salmon, ID 83467
phone: (800) 789-WAVE (9283) • (208) 756-2986 • fax: (208) 756-6373
winter fax: (208) 756-8376 • email: River@IdahoAdventures.com

Join Idaho Adventures for a wilderness whitewater rafting river trip on the Salmon River. We run exciting rapids, camp on sandy beaches, and enjoy our gourmet dining. Our 1 to 3 day trips provide a lively introduction to white water rafting. They are perfect for vacationing families of all ages. If you have time for a longer adventure, choose a 4, 5 or 6 day tour. All are filled the perfect blend of high-powered rapids and calm waters.

Personal gear and an adventurous spirit are all you need to bring; we'll do the rest.

Idaho Adventures has been operating since 1973. Over the years we have learned what makes our guests most comfortable in the wilderness. We've taken care of all the details so all you need to do is fly to Boise and we'll take it from there. Add care and the sheer love of what we do and you will have the most relaxing vacation ever.

"Idaho Adventures guided trip on the Frank Church River of No Return allowed us to "flow with it", accepting its challenges with joy and complete trust in our guides." Eleanor Goodman

SEASONS OF OPERATION

BOAT TYPES

ACTIVITIES

LOCATIONS & SERVICES

Moser's Idaho Adventures

Northwest Voyageurs

Andrew Nachman and Andrew Murray

P.O. Box 373 • Lucile, ID 83542
reservations: (800) 727-9977 • phone: (208) 628-3021 • fax: (208) 628-3780
email: info@voyageurs.com • http://www.voyageurs.com

We take pleasure in turning what you think will be an interesting trip into a once-in-a lifetime experience. We never tire of being told, "There simply aren't words to describe it! Our senses come alive! The thrill was unimaginable."

We're owner-operated, focusing on intimate, quality trips to the best places we know and love. You will quickly understand why more than 70% of the 6,000 plus friends who joined us last year were returning clients or referrals. I personally guarantee you 100% satisfaction!

We use new self-bailing rafts and kayaks, Coast Guard-inspected and -approved life jackets, and waterproof containers for your clothes and cameras. We provide a four-person tent for every two people, plus camp tables and lawn chairs, cocktail ice, refreshing drinks and hors d'oeuvres. After the guides work their culinary magic all waste is packed up and carried out for recycling.

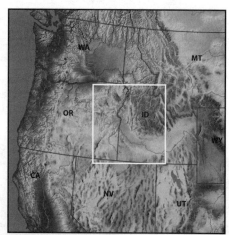

"I never questioned that they'd keep us all safe, entertained, well-fed, and laughing throughout the entire trip." Kristine Schmalz

SEASONS OF OPERATION

BOAT TYPES

ACTIVITIES

LOCATIONS & SERVICES

Rawhide Outfitters

John and Cathy Cranney

204 Larson Street • Salmon, ID 83467
phone: (208) 756-4276 • email: rawhide@salmoninternet.com

Do you savor the opportunity to get away from the crowds, to encounter a canyon and waterway that offers excitement and beauty, or have a quality family experience in nature? The famous Salmon River has much to offer folks of all ages and interests. Its breathtaking scenic beauty, exciting rapids, awesome wildlife, and many interesting historic points make for an unforgettable adventure. It is our goal to see that your river experience surpasses your expectations by catering trips to your personal needs and desires. We own and operate a family outfitting business in the small town of Salmon, Idaho. Our most important concern is to provide a personal, quality, and safe adventure for people who want to enjoy the beautiful outdoors that the Salmon River has to offer.

Come see us, John, Cathy, Justin and Luke at Rawhide Outfitters and we will provide an outdoor adventure that will be the highlight of your vacation!

"I have two teenage sons who loved every single minute of their adventure. England is a long way from Idaho, but a third trip will definitely be planned!" Christine Tibbott, Brighton, England

SEASONS OF OPERATION

BOAT TYPES

ACTIVITIES

LOCATIONS & SERVICES

Rocky Mountain River Tours

Dave and Sheila Mills

P.O. Box 2552 • Boise, ID 83701
phone: (208) 345-2400 • fax: (208) 756-4808 • email: rockymtn@micron.net • www.rafttrip.com
summer: P.O. Box 207 • Salmon, ID 83467 • phone: (208) 756-4808

The primitive, awesome Middle Fork of the Salmon, one of the original eight rivers to be designated Wild and Scenic by Congress in 1980, is still untamed and, for the most part, untouched. Like the Main Salmon, it meanders through the Frank Church River of No Return Wilderness Area. Its whitewater is rated up to Class V in May and June; Class IV in July and August. It's an extraordinary stream, and the outfitters who run it are all top-notch. Even in that company, the six-day, 105-mile trip run by Rocky Mountain River Tours (founded in 1978) stands out.

Owners Dave and Sheila Mills use two paddleboats (accommodating six), four oar boats (accommodating four), and four inflatable single-passenger kayaks. There's one guide for every four guests.

Sheila Mills's Dutch-oven cooking is an essential part of the experience. Exceptional food belongs in this exceptional environment.

"This company was our 3rd on the Middle Fork & definitely the best!" McSwain Family

SEASONS OF OPERATION

BOAT TYPES

ACTIVITIES

LOCATIONS & SERVICES

Silver Cloud Expeditions

Jerry and Terry Myers

P.O. Box 1006 • Salmon, ID 83467
phone: toll free (877) 756-6215 • (208) 756-6215 • fax: (208) 756-6215
email: jmyers@salmoninternet.com • www.silvercloudexp.com

Silver Cloud Expeditions offers top quality five (5) or six (6) day summer wilderness white water vacations on Idaho's spectacular Salmon River through the River of No Return Wilderness.

Owned and operated by Jerry and Terry Myers since 1982, Silver Cloud offers first class access to the 80-mile wild section of the Salmon River in central Idaho.

Natural history and activities are emphasized with experienced guides teaching flora and fauna, native history, night sky, geology, kayaking skills, dutch-oven cooking, fly fishing and gold panning. The river offers big Class 3 (three) rapids, clear cool water, rugged scenery, beautiful white sand beaches, numerous side creeks, hiking trails, historic sites, wildlife, hot springs, ponderosa and fir forests, and shady camps. Enjoy western gourmet meals and comfortably appointed campsites.

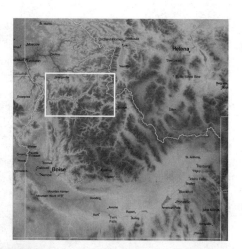

"Jerry Myers has a thorough and respectful understanding of the river's ecosystem & environment, which he shares with gracious western hospitality and warm friendship." Mark Pynn, Ketchum, ID

SEASONS OF OPERATION

BOAT TYPES

ACTIVITIES

LOCATIONS & SERVICES

Silver Cloud
Expeditions

Solitude River Trips

Al and Jeana Bukowsky

main office: P.O. Box 907 • Merlin, OR 97532
summer (June, July, August): PO Box 702, Salmon, ID 83467
phone: (800) 396-1776 • (541) 479-1876 • fax: (541) 471-2235 • www.rivertrips.com

Idaho's Middle Fork of the Salmon River is spectacular beyond imagination.

It carves and churns through 105 miles of the most rugged, inaccessible and primitive country in the United States — a country still relatively untouched by man. There are no roads. It's wild and untamed.

Our guides are licensed professionals with years of boating and fly fishing experience. Solitude River Trips is a bonded, licensed outfitter and guide service.

Without roads, and with limited trail access due to the canyon's rugged nature, the Middle Fork is best seen, explored and fished by floating the river. It is truly a wondrous journey.

Come join us and share the spirit of adventure.

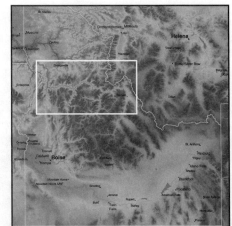

"If there was a rating higher than outstanding, I would have marked that instead. Al & Jeana run a 5-star outfit!"
Shelly Smith

SEASONS OF OPERATION

SPRING | SUMMER | FALL

BOAT TYPES

RAFT | INFLATABLE KAYAK | McKENZIE / DORY | CLASS 2 DIFFICULTY II | CLASS 3 DIFFICULTY III | CLASS 4 DIFFICULTY IV

ACTIVITIES

FLY FISHING | HIKING / TREKKING | ARCHEOLOGICAL SITES | HOT SPRINGS | BIRD WATCHING | WHITEWATER TRIPS | WHITEWATER FISHING | RAFT FISHING

LOCATIONS & SERVICES

BLUE RIBBON WATERS | DOME / SPIKE TENT | KIDS PROGRAMS | FAMILY | HANDICAP | SENIOR CITIZEN | AGE + FULL BOARD | GUIDED ACTIVITIES | OVERNIGHT TRIPS

Solitude

Wapiti River Guides

Gary Lane
P.O. Box 1125 • Riggins, ID 83549
phone: (800) 488-9872 • (208) 628-3523 • fax: (208) 628-3523
email: wapitirg@cyberhighway.net

Wapiti River Guides owner Gary Lane is a modern-day mountain/river man — a tipi dweller living close to nature — who offers new meaning to offbeat trips. If you enjoy wilderness folklore, natural history, close nature encounters and a unique experience led by a trained wildlife biologist, then this trip is for you and your family. Trips are conducted with a combination of whitewater dory, raft, and inflatable kayaks. Rapids range from Class III-V on Idaho's Lower Salmon and Oregon's Grand Ronde and Owyhee rivers. Each journey is strictly limited to small groups. If you wish for solitude, personalized experiences and time away from mass transit affairs, come with Wapiti. Why flock with magpies when you can soar with eagles?

Trips from half to several days' duration offer chukar hunting and steelhead and fly fishing. Specialized workshops include primitive survival skills, yoga and outdoor education.

"Gary Lane's life philosophy is so in tune with nature and his environment that one is totally immersed in the experience and emerges refreshed!" Roy & Kristi Wilson

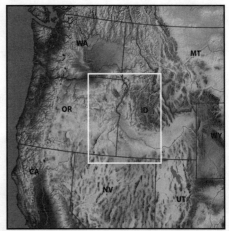

SEASONS OF OPERATION

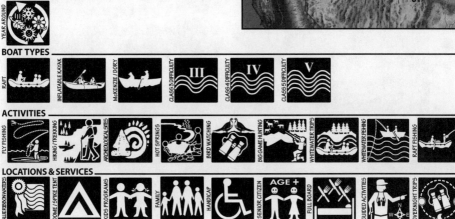

BOAT TYPES

ACTIVITIES

LOCATIONS & SERVICES

Warren River Expeditions, Inc.

David Warren

P.O. Box 1375 • Salmon, ID 83467
phone: (800) 765-0421 • (208) 756-6387 • (208) 756-4495 • fax: (208) 756-3910
email: *salmonriver@raftidaho.com* • *http://www.raftidaho.com*

If you have ever wanted to take a whitewater rafting trip but didn't want to camp out, Warren River Expeditions, Inc. has the perfect trip for you.

Spend six days in Idaho's Frank Church River of No Return Wilderness and on the Main Salmon River.

You will run exciting whitewater and spend each night in a different backcountry lodge. It is a very unique trip and one you will remember always.

While on the river we have the excitement of a whitewater river trip with fishing, hiking, horseback riding and all the adventure of a wilderness trip, with a few amenities of home.

"The food was above & beyond what anyone would expect, and all the equipment was in perfect condition. I would recommend this outfitter to everyone...I have already booked my next trip!"
Connie Eliott

SEASONS OF OPERATION

BOAT TYPES

ACTIVITIES

LOCATIONS & SERVICES

Warren River Expeditions

Kentucky

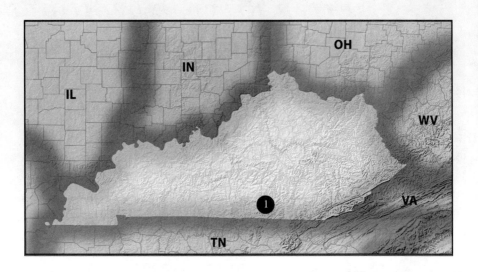

Outdoor Professionals

❶ Sheltowee Trace Outfitters

Useful information for the state of

Kentucky

State and Federal Agencies

Dept. of Fish &Wildlife
#1 Game Farm Rd.
Frankfort, KY 40601
phone: (502) 564-4336

Kentucky Fish & Game
phone: (502) 564-3400

Forest Service
Southern Region
1720 Peachtree Road NW
Atlanta, GA 30367
phone: (404) 347-4177
TTY: (404) 347-4278

Daniel Boone National Forest
1700 Bypass Road
Winchester, KY 40391
phone: (606) 745-3100

Bureau of Land Management
Eastern States
7450 Boston Boulevard
Springfield, VA 22153
phone: (703) 440-1660
or (703) 440- Plus Extension
fax: (703) 440-1599

Office Hours: 8:00 a.m. - 4:30 p.m.

Eastern States
Jackson Field Office
411 Briarwood Drive, Suite 404
Jackson, MS 39206
phone: (601) 977-5400
fax: (601) 977-5440

National Parks

Mammoth Cave National Park
Mammoth Cave, KY 42259
phone: (502) 758-2328

Associations, Publications, etc.

Elkhorn Paddlers
931 South Preston St.
Louisville, KY 40203

License and Report Requirements

- State requires all guides and outfitters to be licensed.

Sheltowee Trace Outfitters

Rick Egedi

P.O. Box 1060 • Whitely City, KY 42653
phone: (800) 541-RAFT (7238) • fax: (606) 528-8779
email: fun@ky-rafting.com • www.ky-rafting.com

Sheltowee Trace Outfitters is located in the middle of the Daniel Boone National Forest in southcentral Kentucky.

Area activities include: whitewater rafting, canoeing, hiking/biking trails, horseback riding, museums, restored historical towns, and more.

Guided raft trips:
BEGINNER (Class III — summer) Ideal for families with children 6 and up or beginners. More than an easy float, but still a mild raft trip. *INTERMEDIATE* (Class IV — spring and fall) These trips offer fantastic whitewater and beautiful scenery. Both a must for whitewater junkies. *EXTREME* (Class V+ — fall) This river is for extremely serious and experienced paddlers only. Two class V paddle runs and ability to self-rescue required.

Unguided Canoe Trips:
Canoe trips can range from half-day to three to four days.

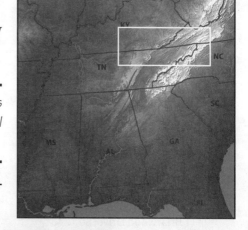

"Sheltowee was excellent...they gave us the most memorable day rafting...! I highly recommend them!" Ray Best

SEASONS OF OPERATION

BOAT TYPES

ACTIVITIES

LOCATIONS & SERVICES

106

Sheltowee Trace Outfitters

Maine

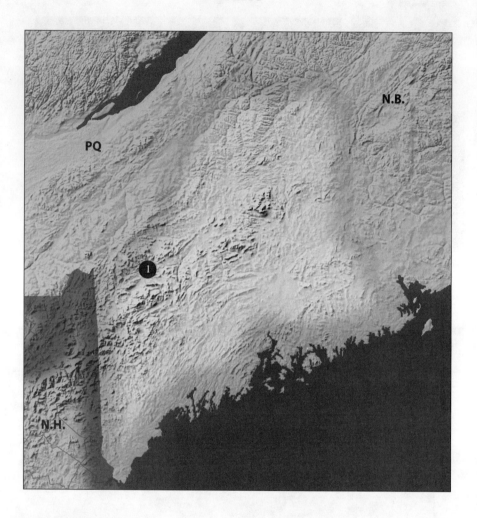

Outdoor Professionals

① Unicorn Rafting Expeditions

License and Report Requirements

• State requires licensing of Outdoor Professionals.

• Monthly Head Fee Guides Report required for Whitewater River Companies.

• No report required for Hunting and Fishing Professionals.

Maine

State and Federal Agencies

Maine Dept. of Fish & Wildlife
284 State St. Station #41
Augusta, ME 04333
phone: (207) 287-8000
fax: (207) 287-6395

Forest Service
Eastern Region
310 West Wisconsin Ave. Rm 500
Milwaukee, WI 53203
phone: (414) 297-3646
TTY: (414) 297-3507

White Mountain National Forest
Federal Building
719 Main Street
Laconia, NH 03246
phone: (603) 528-8721

Bureau of Land Management
Eastern States
7450 Boston Boulevard
Springfield, VA 22153
phone: (703) 440-1660
or (703) 440- Plus Extension
fax: (703) 440-1599

Office Hours: 8:00 a.m. - 4:30 p.m.

Eastern States
Milwaukee District Office
310 W. Wisconsin Ave., Suite 450
(P.O. Box 631 53201-0631)
Milwaukee, WI 53203
phone: (414) 297-4450
fax: (414) 297-4409

National Parks

Acadia National Park
phone: (207) 288-3338

Associations, Publications, etc.

Penobscot Paddle & Chowder Co.
1115 N. Main Street
Brewer, ME 04412
phone: (207) 989-3878

Trout Unlimited Maine Council
President: Dick Walthers
75 Bow Street
Otisfield, ME 04270
phone: (207) 743-7461

Federation of Fly Fishers
http://www.fedflyfishers.org

Atlantic Salmon Commission
650 State St.
Bangor, ME 04401-5654
phone: (207) 941-4449
fax: (207) 941-4443

American Bass Assoc. of Maine
20 Marshwood Estates
Eliot, ME 03903
phone: (207) 748-1744

Sportsman's Alliance of Maine
RR 1, Box 1174
Church Hill Road
Augusta, ME 04330-9749
phone: (207) 622-5503
fax: (207) 622-5596

Maine Bass Chapter Federation
RR 1. Box 332
Hollis Center, ME 04042
phone: (207) 929-8553

Maine Professional Guide Association
phone: (207) 549-5631 or 549-4579

The Maine Sportsman
phone: (207) 846-9501

Unicorn Rafting Expeditions

Jay Schurman

Rt. 201 • Lake Parlin, ME 04945
phone: (800) UNICORN (864-2676) • (207) 668-7629 • fax: (207) 668-7627
email: rafting@maine.com • www.unicornraft.com

Whether you are looking for a family wilderness canoe trip or a heart-pounding journey through Magic Falls or Cribwork Rapids, Unicorn has an adventure with you in mind.

We operate from a simple philosophy: we treat our guests as family. Your safety and enjoyment are as important to us as our own children's welfare.

For more than 18 years we have been committed to offering the finest adventures in New England. This process includes providing the best trained and friendliest guides at the best adventure resorts on the Kennebec, Dead and Penobscot rivers.

We are the only river outfitter in New England with enough confidence in our programs to guarantee our outdoor adventures.

"... our guides went out of their way to provide my family with an outstanding adventure that we will remember fondly!"
Donald Rice

SEASONS OF OPERATION

BOAT TYPES

ACTIVITIES

LOCATIONS & SERVICES

Unicorn Rafting Expeditions

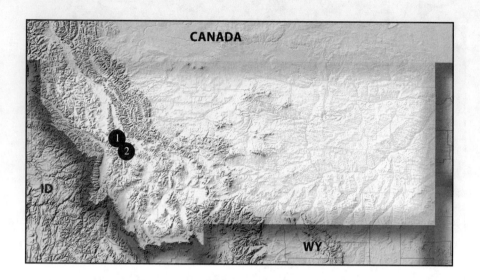

Outdoor Professionals

1. Western Waters & Woods
2. Wild Rockies Tours

License and Report Requirements

• State requires licensing of Outdoor Professionals.

• State requires an "Annual Client Report Log" for all Hunting and Fishing Outfitters.

• State does not regulate River Guides.

• Guest/Dude Ranches need to get an Outfitter license only if they take guest to fish or hunt on land that they do not own.

Useful information for the state of

Montana

State and Federal Agencies

Montana Board of Outfitters
Dept. of Commerce
Arcade Building - 111 North Jackson
Helena, MT 59620-0407
phone: (406) 444-3738

Montana Dept. of Fish, Wildlife & Parks
1420 East 6th
Helena, MT 59620
phone: (406) 444-2535

Forest Service
Northern Region
Federal Building
PO Box 7669
Missoula, MT 59807-7669
phone: (406) 329-3616
TTY: (406) 329-3510

Bitterroot National Forest
phone: (406) 363-3131

Custer National Forest
phone / TTY: (406) 248-9885

Flathead National Forest
phone: (406) 755-5401

Gallatin National Forest
phone / TTY: (406) 587-6920
fax: (406) 587-6758

Helena National Forest
phone: (406) 449-5201

Kootenai National Forest
phone: (406) 293-6211

Lewis & Clark National Forest
phone: (406) 791-7700

Lolo National Forest
phone: (406) 329-3750

Bureau of Land Management
Montana State Office
Granite Tower
222 North 32nd Street
P.O. Box 36800
Billings, MT 59107-6800
phone: (406) 255-2885
fax: (406) 255-2762
Email - mtinfo@mt.blm.gov
Office Hours: 8:00 a.m. - 4:30 p.m.

National Parks

Glacier National Park
phone: (406) 888-5441

Associations, Publications, etc.

Flathead Whitewater Association, Inc.
PO Box 114
Whitefish, MT 59937
phone: (406) 862-2386

Fishing Outfitters Assoc. of Montana
PO Box 67
Gallatin Gateway, MT 59730
phone: (406) 763-5436

Federation of Fly Fishers
PO Box 1595
502 South 19th, Ste. #1
Bozeman, MT 59771
phone: (406) 585-7592
fax: (406) 585-7596
http://www.fedflyfishers.org

Trout Unlimited Montana Council
Council Chairman: Michael A. Bushly
2611 - 5th Avenue South
Great Falls, MT 59405-3023
phone: (406) 727-8787
fax: (406) 727-2402
Email: mbushly@cmrussell.org
http://www.montanatu.org

Montana Bass Chapter Federation
12345 O'Keefe Road
Missoula, MT 59812
phone: (406) 728-8842

Western Waters and Woods

Jerry Nichols

5455 Keil Loop • Missoula, MT 59802
phone: (800) 757-1680 PIN #2060 • (406) 543-3203
email: waters@bigsky.net • http://www.bigsky.net/westernwaters

Western Waters and Woods is a family-owned guide and outfitter service established in 1976 by Montana native Gerald R. Nichols.

We operate as a whitewater, fishing, charter boat, and hunting guide service based in Missoula, Montana.

I take great pride in being a state-licensed outfitter, and offer day or extended trips in Montana and Alaska.

We float the whitewater and fish the blue ribbon trout streams of Montana. We are the original outfitter of whitewater float trips through the now-famous Alberton Gorge on the Clark Fork River.

The Clark Fork, Madison, Big Hole and Missouri Rivers offer breathtaking white-water and trophy trout fishing.

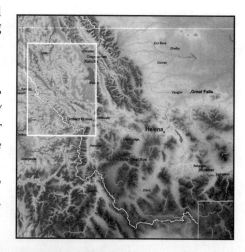

"Jerry's knowledge and skill level are only found in someone who has spent their lives on and around rivers...one of the best!" Rich Rose

SEASONS OF OPERATION

BOAT TYPES

ACTIVITIES

LOCATIONS & SERVICES

Wild Rockies Tours

Gail Gutsche, Matt Thomas, Dan Ward

P.O. Box 8184 • Missoula, MT 59807
phone: (406) 728-0566 • fax: (406) 728-4134
email: gutsche@wildrockies.org

Wild Rockies Tours specializes in three- to eight-day canoe trips on the Missouri, Yellowstone, Clark Fork and Blackfoot Rivers, located in beautiful Montana. Opportunities for wildlife viewing are frequent and often thrilling. Birding is spectacular; sightings of bald and golden eagles are common. Our small group tours — minimum of four, maximum of eight — assures that our guests receive plenty of personal attention and allows us to travel lightly on the land. Tasty camp meals, first-rate equipment and trained guides provided. Custom tours and mountaineering trips available on request.

Celebrate Lewis and Clark's famous expedition. This eight-day canoe tour of the Wild and Scenic Missouri River features mild paddling through the remote Missouri Breaks and White Cliffs, which has changed little since the time of the famous captains.

NOTE: We do not fish or raft.

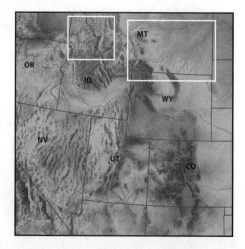

"It was an adventure of a lifetime! Our comfort and security were top priorities at all times!" Robert Ward

SEASONS OF OPERATION

BOAT TYPES

ACTIVITIES

LOCATIONS & SERVICES

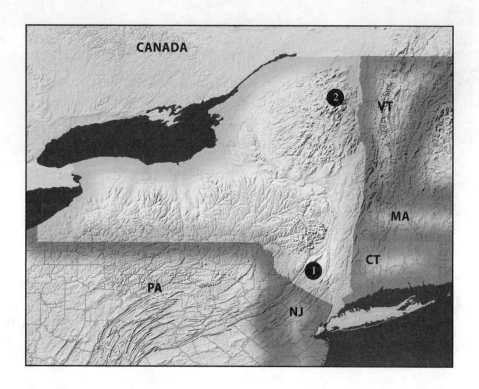

Outdoor Professionals

1. Earth River Expeditions
2. Middle Earth Expeditions

New York

State and Federal Agencies

Dept. of Environmental Conservation
50 Wolf Rd.
Albany, NY 12233
phone: (518) 457-3400

Bureau of Land Management
Eastern States
7450 Boston Boulevard
Springfield, VA 22153
phone: (703) 440-1660
or (703) 440- Plus Extension
fax: (703) 440-1599

Office Hours: 8:00 a.m. - 4:30 p.m.

Eastern States
Milwaukee District Office
310 W. Wisconsin Ave., Suite 450
(P.O. Box 631 53201-0631)
Milwaukee, WI 53203
phone: (414) 297-4450
fax: (414) 297-4409

Fire Island National Seashore
120 Laurel Street
Patchogue, NY 11772
phone: (631) 475-1665

Finger Lakes National Forest
5218 State Route 414
Hector, NY 14841
phone: (607-456-4470
fax: (607) 546-4474

Associations, Publications, etc.

Trout Unlimited New York Council
2711 Girdle Road
Elma, NY 14059
phone: (716) 655-1331 or (914) 892-8630

American Fisheries Society
Cornell Biological Field Station
R.D. 1
Bridgeport, NY 13030
phone: (315) 633-9243

Federation of Fly Fishers
http://www.fedflyfishers.org

Great Lakes Sport Fishing Council
PO Box 297
Elmhurst, IL 60126
phone: (630) 941-1351
fax: (630) 941-1196
email: glsfc@netwave.net
http://www.execpc.com/glsfc

New York Bass Chapter Federation
274 N. Goodman Street
Rochester, NY 14607
phone: (716) 271-7000

New York State Outdoor Guides Assoc.
(NYSOGA)
PO Box 4704
Queensbury, NY 12804
phone: (518) 359-7037
phone/fax: (518) 798-1253

License and Report Requirements

• State requires licensing of Guides.

• State requires that Guides be re-certified each year.

• State has no report requirements.

Earth River Expeditions

Eric Hertz, President

P.O. Box 182A • Accord, NY 12404
phone: (800) 643-2784 • (914) 626-2665 • fax: (914) 626-4423
www.earthriver.com

Earth River Expeditions takes people to some of the wildest and most remote places in the world. Using rivers as our primary means of transportation allows us to reach wonderful places beyond the boundaries of normal travel.

During the past few years, Earth River has pioneered commercial rafting on a number of classic rivers, including Chile's magnificent Futaleufu, Peru's two-mile deep Colen River Canyon, Canada's pristine Magpie, and China's exotic Great Bend of the Yangtze.

When running wild rivers in remote places, it is important to receive the safest trip possible. No one is more conscientious. We use the safest techniques presently being used on difficult rivers throughout the world.

"Earth River is by far the best outfitter I've been with in terms of what really matters… knowledge of the water, exceptional training, concerns for safety and relentless attention to detail!" Bill Fair

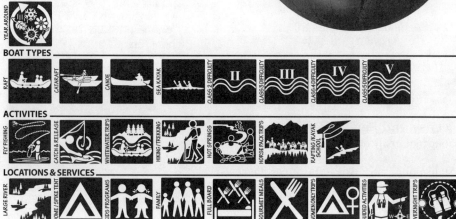

SEASONS OF OPERATION

YEAR AROUND

BOAT TYPES

RAFT | CATARAFT | CANOE | SEA KAYAK | CLASS 2 DIFFICULTY II | CLASS 3 DIFFICULTY III | CLASS 4 DIFFICULTY IV | CLASS 5 DIFFICULTY V

ACTIVITIES

FLY FISHING | CATCH & RELEASE | WHITEWATER TRIPS | HIKING/TREKKING | HOT SPRINGS | HORSE PACK TRIPS | RAFTING/KAYAK SCHOOL

LOCATIONS & SERVICES

LARGE RIVER | DOME/SPIKE TENT | KIDS PROGRAMS | FAMILY | FULL BOARD | GOURMET MEALS | WOMEN ONLY TRIPS | GUIDED ACTIVITIES | OVERNIGHT TRIPS

Middle Earth Expeditions

Wayne Failing

HCR 01, Box 37—Rt. 73 • Lake Placid, NY 12946-9702
phone: (518) 523-9572
email: wayne2@northnet.org • www.adirondackrafting.com

The Adirondack Mountains, declared "forever wild" by the New York State Legislature in 1885, cover some 6 million acres of land and waterways.

This is the setting for Middle Earth Expeditions, led by outdoorsman, photographer and philosopher Wayne Failing, a founding member of the Hudson River Professional Outfitters Association. Some of the most challenging and exciting whitewater in the Northeast can be found on the Hudson River. This 17-mile river trip through remote wilderness areas will have you crashing through whitewater rapids (class III, IV, V) one moment and enjoying the magnificent scenery from gentle pools the next. We specialize in personal small-group rafting adventures with a professional Adirondack guide to teach you whitewater skills and share his knowledge of the river's natural history. Other river trips, fishing floats, and two and three day overnights are also available.

"A sincere, interesting, experienced man....a story teller, singer, guitarist, outdoorsman, born teacher.....add the great outdoors and you have an incredible winning experience!" Sy Balsen

SEASONS OF OPERATION

BOAT TYPES

ACTIVITIES

LOCATIONS & SERVICES

Top Rated Professionals in
Oregon

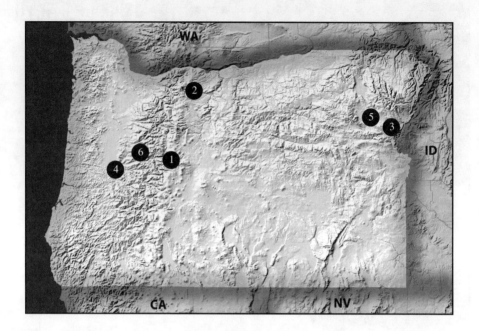

Outdoor Professionals

1. Chinook Whitewater
2. Ewing's Whitewater
3. Hells Canyon Adventures
4. Outdoor Ventures
5. Peer's Snake River Rafting
6. Tightlines

License and Report Requirements

- State requires licensing of Outdoor Professionals.
- State requires a "Year-End Report" for Outfitters hunting and/or fishing on BLM land.
- U.S. Coast Guard licensing required for guides and captains who fish in "Near Coastal Waters".

State and Federal Agencies

Oregon Dept. of Fish & Wildlife
PO Box 59
Portland, OR 97207
phone: (503) 872-5268

Oregon Marine Board
435 Commercial St. NE
Salem, OR 97310
phone: (503) 373-1405
or (503) 378-8587

Columbia River Gorge Ntl. Scenic Area
902 Wasco Avenue, Ste 200
Hood River, OR 97031
phone: (541) 386-2333

Forest Service
Pacific Northwest Region
333 SW 1st Avenue
PO Box 3623
Portland, OR 97208
phone: (503) 326-2971
TTY: (503) 326-6448

Rogue River National Forest
phone: (541) 858-2200

Siskiyou National Forest
phone: (541) 471-6500

Siuslaw National Forest
phone: (541) 750-7000

Umpqua National Forest
phone: (541) 672-6601

Winema National Forest
phone: (541) 883-6714

Bureau of Land Management
Oregon State Office
1515 SW 5th Ave.
P.O. Box 2965
Portland, OR 97208-2965
phone: (503) 952-6001
or (503) 952-Plus Extension
fax: (503) 952-6308
Tdd: (503) 952-6372

Electronic mail
General Information:
or912mb@or.blm.gov
Webmaster: orwww@or.blm.gov

National Parks

Crater Lake National Park
PO Box 7
Crater Lake, OR 97604
phone: (541) 594-2211

Associations, Publications, etc.

Oregon Outdoor Association
PO Box 9486
Bend, OR 97708-9486
phone: (541) 382-9758

Gorge Whitewater Paddlers Assoc.
105 Oak Street
Hood River, OR 97031
phone: (541) 387-3527

Southern Oregon Paddlers
PO Box 2111
Bandon, OR 97411
phone: (541) 347-3480

South Oregon Assoc. of Kayakers
1951 Roberts Road
Medford, OR 97504
phone: (541) 772-4762

Chinook Whitewater

Tim Thornton

PO Box 7962 • Bend, OR 97708
phone: (800) 226-1001 • (541) 383-1460 • email: ttrd@europa.com

Chinook Whitewater is the Northwest's premier outfitter focusing on personal river trips. Our small company attitude provides our guests with unforgettable adventures of a lifetime. Our trips cater to every ability, age, and special occasion. The moods of our trips are informal and intimate. Our primary goal is simply to provide the best possible river experience.

Imagine escaping reality and playing on some of the Northwest's most magical rivers. The daily hustle and bustle, telephones, computers and traffic are completely left at home. Solitude, scenery, fresh air, good people and most importantly, relaxation, soon take over. Our trips range from half-day quickies to full seven-day adventures.

A new partnership has allowed us to offer trips on the Clackamas and White Salmon Rivers. Add these two rivers to our great existing menu and this is a serious recipe for an unforgettable experience.

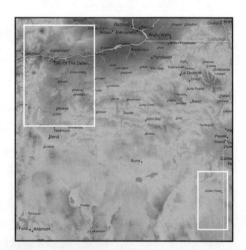

"We had a wonderful time! Our guide was excellent, he really made our trip!"
Shannon Fasold

SEASONS OF OPERATION

BOAT TYPES

ACTIVITIES

LOCATIONS & SERVICES

CHINOOK
WHITEWATER

Ewing's Whitewater

Pete Hattenhauer

P.O. Box 265 • Maupin, OR 97037
phone: (800) 538-RAFT (7238) • fax: (541) 395-2657

Specializing in one- to three-day whitewater vacations, Ewing's strives to enhance it's clients' appreciation of a quality outdoor adventure. The experience of a lifetime awaits in the Deschutes River corridor. This natural landscape of high desert canyon views with craggy basalt outcroppings and spectacular sage and juniper draped drainages, is amazingly awesome. As the Deschutes cuts its path through these majestic views, exciting and thrilling whitewater await around every bend. Relaxation is at its peak in this serene, scenic masterpiece of cascading rapids and unbelievable ruggedness. It is our privilege to entertain our guests in such a grand environment. By providing first-class adventure tours, Ewing's has taken professionalism to new heights. From our gourmet riverside cuisine to our seasoned staff, the extra mile is common practice for our guests.

Word-of-mouth has always been our best advertising — for good reason.

"When Ewing's Whitewater was given the added challenge of someone physically handicapped on the trip, Pete and his staff rose to the occasion with great professionalism and compassion; never do I remember a more exciting whitewater adventure!" Diane Lindhorst

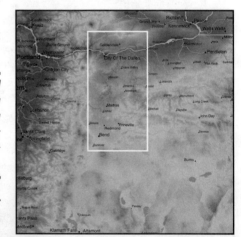

SEASONS OF OPERATION

BOAT TYPES

ACTIVITIES

LOCATIONS & SERVICES

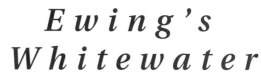

Ewing's
Whitewater

Hells Canyon Adventures

Bret and Doris Armacost

P.O. Box 159 • Oxbow, OR 97840
phone: (800) 422-3568 • (541) 785-3352 • fax: (541) 785-3353
email jetboat@pdx.oneworld.com • Hellscanyonadventures.com

Hells Canyon Adventures has been a family-owned operation since 1983, showing Hells Canyon's deepest points to the public. Our most important type of advertising is **"word-of-mouth from past guests."**

During the summer months, we offer two and three hour jet boat tours for the lighthearted, and six hour tours for the adventurous. In the fall and spring we offer a two-day tour with an overnight in Lewiston, Idaho. We also offer on request, off-season jet boat tours, drop camps for hunting and fishing, jet-backs for floaters, and steelhead fishing and chukar hunting from fall to early spring.

For an all-out adventure, we suggest a one-day whitewater rafting excursion. We'll raft Hells Canyon's best rapids and return upstream by jet boat the same day, giving you a second chance to see all the big rapids.

"Bret has always been very professional and cautious about the safety of his clients. I regularly recommend Hells Canyon Adventures to my friends!" Joe McDonald

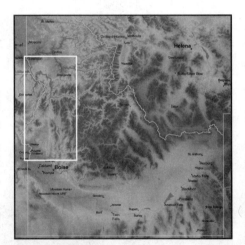

SEASONS OF OPERATION

BOAT TYPES

ACTIVITIES

LOCATIONS & SERVICES

Outdoor Ventures River Training & Registry

Robb Grubb and William Blair

P.O. Box 25736 • Eugene, OR   97402
phone: (541) 683-7428 • fax: (541) 683-0775
email: training@infraspect.com • http://www.infraspect.com

Become river people! OutdoorVentures offers you an extensive multi-day fishing and whitewater guide program, as well as day-long training courses for the private boater. Each of our guide/instructors have over 15+ years of river running experience.

We specialize in small group and "one-on-one" training in dories, rafts (rowing & paddling), drift boats and catarafts. We can also train you in your own boat. This is fun, in-depth, educational river running. We are conveniently based out of Eugene, Oregon near many rivers that have an excellent variety of characteristics and difficulty to fulfill your training curriculum. Our guide Registry offers a professional portfolio of competency on the water and potentially lower insurance rates.

OutdoorVentures welcomes you to come and learn the river skills that will keep yourself, your family and your guests safe while fishing or at play.

"I would recommend them to anyone wanting any river experience from mild to wild, and river training from beginner to guide instructor. There is no substitute for their knowledge and experience." Andy Hardwich, Salem, OR

SEASONS OF OPERATION

BOAT TYPES

ACTIVITIES

LOCATIONS & SERVICES

Peer's Snake River Rafting

Darryl and Kathy Peer

P.O. Box 354 • 263 West Record St. • Halfway, OR 97834
phone: (800) 555-0005 • (541) 742-2050
email: rafting@pinetel.com • www.neoregon.net/peersrafting

Come raft the mighty Snake River of Hells Canyon—the deepest canyon in North America. While you are here, you'll experience some of the best whitewater rapids in the United States.

Our guides will propel you down the river on 18' rafts, or you may choose to be directly involved with the "u-paddle" option, where everyone paddles, or challenge the rapids on your own by slipping into one of our inflatable kayaks. Fishing is great on the Snake River. Trout and bass are plentiful here, or you may want to fish for sturgeon, a large, prehistoric bottom fish. After your day on the river, relax at our deluxe camp. We pride ourselves on the quality of our menu, where meals are prepared with the freshest foods in a fine, western manner.

Naturally, we are happy to include any special dietary requirements. Refresh and rejuvenate your spirit with the beauty and power of Hells Canyon with Peer's Snake River Rafting.

"...had more fun & satisfaction than any river trip I've been on. The Peer Family is great!! I'll be back!" Don W. Emerson, Centerville, MO

SEASONS OF OPERATION

BOAT TYPES

ACTIVITIES

LOCATIONS & SERVICES

PSRR

Tightlines

Jeff and Laura Helfrich

47611 McKenzie Highway • Vida, OR 97488
phone/fax: (541) 896-3219 • email: FishOR9446@aol.com

A family business since the early 1920s, Tightlines offers safety-oriented family trips on Oregon's McKenzie, Rogue, Owyhee and Idaho's Salmon Rivers. From one (1) to five (5) days our journeys take you through some of the most beautiful awe-inspiring scenery in North America accessible only by river or trail. A luxurious riverside camp ends your day of whitewater relaxation. Gourmet foods such as dutch-oven baked breads, meats grilled over open fire and freshly prepared salads means there's no room for dieting. Swimming, hiking, fishing, and relaxing are some of the activities you may choose to fulfill each day. Our guides are not only experienced oarsmen but great cooks and will share with you their knowledge on fishing, river history, geology, and archeology during each day's float.

We want you to have a great time on your vacation and go home looking forward to joining us again.

"I wholeheartedly recommend Tightlines river trips. Guides are skillful, mature & safety conscious..they also make sure that guests have fun! We shall certainly go on Tightlines trips again!"
Terry Salter-Haag, Sebastobol, CA

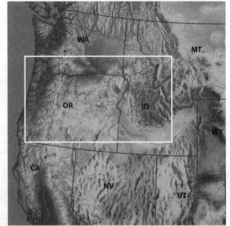

SEASONS OF OPERATION

SPRING · SUMMER · FALL

BOAT TYPES

RAFT · INFLATABLE KAYAK · McKENZIE / DORY · CLASS 1 DIFFICULTY **I** · CLASS 2 DIFFICULTY **II** · CLASS 3 DIFFICULTY **III** · CLASS 4 DIFFICULTY **IV**

ACTIVITIES

FLY FISHING · WHITEWATER TRIPS · WILDLIFE VIEWING · SPIN CASTING · CATCH & RELEASE · HIKING / TREKKING · RAFT FISHING · ARCHEOLOGICAL SITES · HOT SPRINGS

LOCATIONS & SERVICES

BLUE RIBBON STREAM · LARGE RIVER · LODGE · DOME / SPIKE TENT · FAMILY · WOMEN ONLY TRIPS · GUIDED ACTIVITIES · OVERNIGHT TRIPS

Tightlines

Pennsylvania

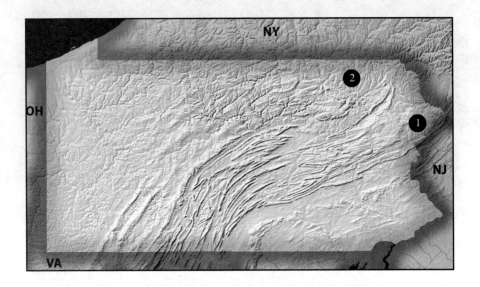

Outdoor Professionals

1. Kittatinny Canoes
2. Pine Creek Outfitters, Inc.

License and Report Requirements

• State requires licensing of Outdoor Professionals.

• State requires the filing of the "Charter Boat/Fishing Guide Report".

Pennsylvania

State and Federal Agencies

Pennsylvania Game Commission
PO Box 67000
Harrisburg, PA 17110
hunting: (717) 787-4250
fishing: (717) 657-4518

Division of Tourism
Commonwealth of Pennsylvania
phone: (800) 847-4872

Forest Service
Eastern Region
310 West Wisconsin Avenue, Room 500
Milwaukee, WI 53203
phone: (414) 297-3646
TTY: (414) 297-3507

Allegheny National Forest
222 Liberty Street
PO Box 847
Warren, PA 16365
phone: (814) 723-5150
TTY: (814) 726-2710

Bureau of Land Management
Eastern States
7450 Boston Boulevard
Springfield, VA 22153
phone: (703) 440-1600
or (703) 440- Plus Extension
fax: (703) 440-1599

Office Hours: 8:00 a.m. - 4:30 p.m.

Eastern States
Milwaukee District Office
310 W. Wisconsin Ave., Suite 450
(P.O. Box 631 53201-0631)
Milwaukee, WI 53203
phone: (414) 297-4450
fax: (414) 297-4409

Associations, Publications, etc.

Western Pennsylvania Paddle Sport
Association
110 Thornwood Lane
Slippery Rock, PA 16057
phone: (412) 735-2833

Wildwater Boating Club
118 E. South Hills Avenue
State College, PA 16801
phone: (814) 237-7727

Trout Unlimited Pennsylvania Council
President: Melvin S. Brown
239 Station Road
Fairfield, PA 17320
phone: (717) 642-2449
fax: (717) 642-2475
Email: mel.brown@quebecorusa.com

Federation of Fly Fishers
http://www.fedflyfishers.org

Pennsylvania Bass Chapter Fed., Inc.
769 N. Cottage Road
Mercer, PA 16137
phone: (412) 475-2422
http://www.pabass.com

Great Lakes Sport Fishing Council
PO Box 297
Elmhurst, IL 60126
phone: (630) 941-1351
fax: (630) 941-1196
email: glsfc@netwave.net
http://www.execpc.com/glsfc

North American Native Fisheries Assoc.
123 W. Mt. Airy Ave.
Philadelphia, PA 19119

Kittatinny Canoes

Dave and Ruth Jones

HC 67 Box 360, Silver Lake Rd. • Dingmans Ferry, PA 18328
phone: (800) FLOAT-KC (356-2582) • (717) 828-2338 • fax: (717) 828-2165
www.kittatinny.com

A Kittatinny River adventure is just what you need! It's wilderness nearby, fun, excitement, and laughter. It's picnicking, swimming, sunbathing and relaxing with the sights and sounds of nature.

The Delaware is a designated National Scenic and Recreational River managed by the National Park Service. Crystal-clear water, spectacular rock formations, lush forested mountains and abundant wildlife will place you in the outdoor spirit.

Kittatinny is proud of this unique resource and is committed to its preservation as demonstrated by our award-winning annual river cleanups. We've received numerous awards, including national recognition as a first-place winner in Take Pride in America for two consecutive years, and a Gold Star Award from the National Park Service.

We offer calm and whitewater trips. Kittatinny Canoes is a member of the Professional Paddlesports Association and America Outdoors.

"Learned to Kayak...trip was excellent!"
Nancy Mason

SEASONS OF OPERATION

BOAT TYPES

ACTIVITIES

LOCATIONS & SERVICES

Pine Creek Outfitters, Inc.

Chuck Dillon

RR 4 Box 130B • Wellsboro, PA 16901
phone: (717) 724-3003
email: pinecrk@clarityconnect.com • www.pinecrk.com

Pine Creek Outfitters, Inc. features a one-day, 17-mile guided float trip through Pine Creek Gorge, "the Grand Canyon of Pennsylvania." This section of Pine Creek was designated a National Natural Landmark by the National Park Service in 1968. The gorge is a Pennsylvania State Forest Natural Area and is part of the Pennsylvania Scenic Rivers System.

The trip is participatory, requiring each participant to paddle. Minimum age for the six-hour trip is 7 years old. By the end of the trip each participant will have learned about the geology, forest history and local folklore of the canyon. Chuck Dillon, head guide, recognized local expert, storyteller, and the author of several books on the canyon area, personally leads most trips. Write or call for a free copy of the 20-page "Outdoor Adventure Guide for Grand Canyon of Pennsylvania."

"This trip was excellent family time. I have recommended this trip to several of our friends!"

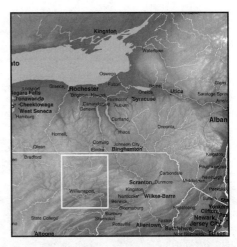

SEASONS OF OPERATION

BOAT TYPES

ACTIVITIES

LOCATIONS & SERVICES

Tennessee

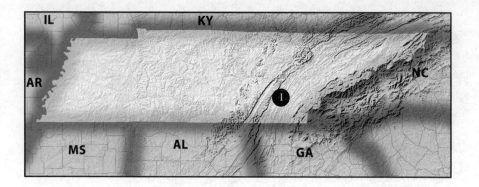

Outdoor Professionals

① Ocoee Outdoors

License and Report Requirements

• State does not license or register Outfitters, Guides, Captains or Lodges.

• State has no report requirements.

Useful information for the state of

Tennessee

State and Federal Agencies

Tennessee Wildlife Resources Agency
PO Box 40747
Ellington Agriculture Center
Nashville, TN 37204
phone: (615) 781-6500

Tennessee Conservation League
phone: (615) 353-1133

Forest Service
Southern Region
1720 Peachtree Road NW
Atlanta, GA 30367
phone: (404) 347-4177
TTY: (404) 347-4278

Cherokee National Forest
2800 North Ocoee Street NE
PO Box 2010
Cleveland, TN 37320
phone: (423) 476-9700
fax: (423) 339-3652

Bureau of Land Management
Eastern States
7450 Boston Boulevard
Springfield, VA 22153
phone: (703) 440-1660
or (703) 440- Plus Extension
fax: (703) 440-1599

Office Hours: 8:00 a.m. - 4:30 p.m.

Eastern States
Jackson Field Office
411 Briarwood Drive, Suite 404
Jackson, MS 39206
phone: (601) 977-5400
fax: (601) 977-5440

National Parks

Great Smoky Mountains National Park
107 Park Headquarters Road
Gatlinburg, TN 37738
phone: (423) 436-1200

Associations, Publications, etc.

America Outdoors
PO Box 10847
Knoxville, TN 37939
phone: (423) 558-3595
fax: (423) 558-3598
Email: infoacct@americaoutdoors.org
http://www.adventuresports.com/ao/
welcome.htm

Ocoee Outdoors

J. T. Lemons

P.O. Box 72 • Ocoee, TN 37361
reservations: (800) 533-PROS (7767) • phone: (423) 338-2438 • fax: (423) 338-6128
www.ocoee-outdoors.com

Go with the pros. Raft America's most popular whitewater river with Ocoee Outdoors, Tennessee's No. 1 river outfitter since 1977. The Ocoee features more than 20 exciting rapids in the 5-mile adventure.

Anyone can meet the Ocoee challenge with the help of the Ocoee's professional guides. Ocoee Outdoors' guides collectively have more than 600 years of whitewater experience, 40,000 trips, and more than 200,000 miles logged on the Ocoee. They are friendly and courteous professionals. We raft the Ocoee, Big Pigeon and Hiwassee Rivers. Ocoee Outdoors' new facilities include change rooms, showers, a gift shop, color photos of your Ocoee River adventure, horseback riding, live music on weekends, and private campground.

We are less than 30 minutes from I-75. For the longest trip on the Ocoee (two hours plus), and the most experienced river guides, call the pros.

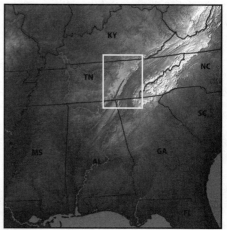

"Our company sponsors a rafting trip for all interested employees each year. We use Ocoee Outdoors every year because of their outstanding reputation. They help to make our trip a very exciting & memorable day."
Mary Bunch/Reliable Heating & A/C Company

SEASONS OF OPERATION

BOAT TYPES

ACTIVITIES

LOCATIONS & SERVICES

Top Rated Professionals in
Utah

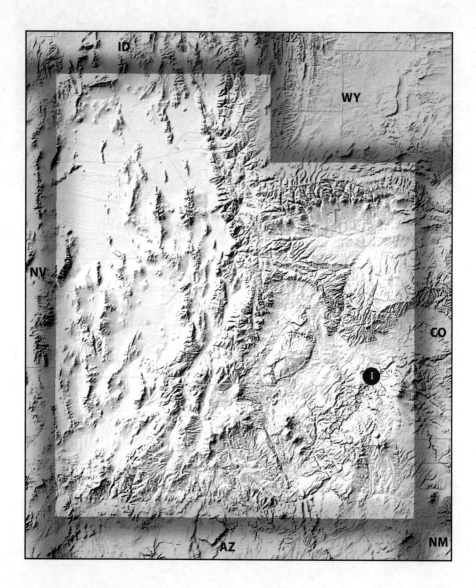

Outdoor Professionals

1 Sheri Griffith Expeditions, Inc.

Useful information for the state of

Utah

State and Federal Agencies

Utah Dept. of Natural Resources
1636 W. North Temple
Salt Lake City, UT 84116
phone: (801) 538-4700

Forest Service
Intermountain Region
324 25th Street
Ogden, UT 84401-2310
phone: (801) 625-5306
TTY: (801) 625-5307

Ashley National Forest
phone: (435) 781-5157

Dixie National Forest
phone: (801) 865-3700

Fishlake National Forest
phone: (801) 638-1033

Manti-LaSal National Forest
phone / TTY: (801) 637-2817

Uinta National Forest
phone: (801) 342-5100

Wasatch-Cache National Forests
phone: (801) 524-3900

Bureau of Land Management
Utah State Office
P.O. Box 45155
Salt Lake City, UT 84145-0155
Information Number: (801) 539-4001
fax: (801) 539-4013
Office Hours: 8:00 a.m. - 4:00 p.m.

National Parks

Arches National Park
Moab, UT 84532
phone: (801) 259-8161

Bryce Canyon National Park
Bryce Canyon, UT 84717
phone: (801) 834-5322

Canyonlands National Park
Moab, UT 84532
phone: (435) 259-7164

Capitol Reef National Park
Torrey, UT 84775
phone: (435) 425-3791

Zion National Park
Springdale, UT 84767
phone: (435) 772-3256

Associations, Publications, etc.

World Wide Outfitter & Guide Assoc.
PO Box 520400
Salt Lake City, UT 84152-0400
phone: (801) 566-2662

Utah Whitewater Club
PO Box 520183
Salt Lake City, UT 84152

License and Report Requirements

• State does not license or register Outfitters, Guides, Captains or Lodges.
• State Parks & Recreation Division requires that River Rafting Guides and Outfitters register and file a "River Outfitting Company Registration".
• BLM, Forest Service and National Park Service require a "Use Permit" and "User Fee" for Boating, Fish and River Outfitters using their lands. Guides and Outfitters required to file a "Year End Report of Activities".

Sheri Griffith Expeditions, Inc.

Sheri Griffith

P.O. Box 1324 • 2231 South Highway 191 • Moab, UT 84532
phone: (800) 332-2439 • (435) 259-8229 • fax: (435) 259-2226
email: classriver@aol.com • www.GriffithExp.com

Enjoy the excitement of the outdoors without the work. Utah river rafting journeys, two- to six-day trips on the Colorado, Green and Dolores Rivers through national parks and wild and scenic stretches.

We make you comfortable in the wilderness and take care of all the details. No experience necessary. Professional guides, state-of-the-art equipment and excellent safety record combine to create an unforgettable experience. Choose from the larger stable rafts to the smaller high-action boats.

This is our 27th year rafting the best rivers of the Southwest. Some specialties include, "Family Goes to Camp," "Women Only," and "Luxury Expeditions," or, let us design a custom trip for you. Free 24-page brochure and video available.

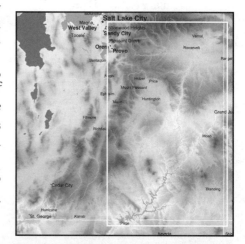

"My father and I agree this was one of our best trips ever. The guides and the people were wonderful, the food was amazing, and the trip overall was incredible!" Maria Marsh and Dad, Joel

SEASONS OF OPERATION

BOAT TYPES

ACTIVITIES

LOCATIONS & SERVICES

Sheri Griffith Expeditions, Inc.

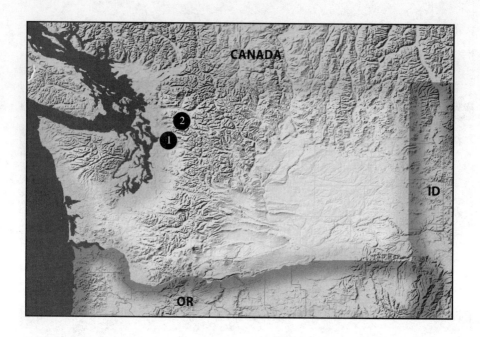

Outdoor Professionals

1. DownStream River Runners, Inc.
2. Redline River Adventures

License and Report Requirements

- State requires licensing of Outdoor Professionals.
- State requires that licensed steelhead guides report any catches.

Washington

State and Federal Agencies

Washington Fish & Wildlife
600 North Capitol Way
Olympia, WA 98501
phone: (360) 902-2200
fax: (360) 902-2300

Forest Service
Pacific Northwest Region
333 SW 1st Avenue
PO Box 3623
Portland, OR 97208
phone: (503) 808-2971

Colville National Forest
phone: (509) 684-7000

Gifford Pinchot National Forest
phone: (360) 891-5000

Mt. Baker-Snoqualmie National Forest
phone: (206) 775-9702

Okanogan National Forest
phone: (509) 826-3275

Olympic National Forest
phone: (360) 956-2300

Wenatchee National Forest
phone: (509) 662-4335

Bureau of Land Management
Oregon State Office
(serves Washington also)
1515 SW 5th Ave.
P.O. Box 2965
Portland, OR 97208-2965
phone: (503) 952-6001
fax: (503) 952-6308

General Information
Email : or912mb@or.blm.gov
Webmaster: orwww@or.blm.gov
Office Hours: 7:30 a.m. - 4:30 p.m.

Spokane District Office
1103 N. Fancher
Spokane, WA 99212
phone: (509) 536-1200
fax: (509) 536-1275
Email: or130mb@or.blm.gov

National Parks

Mount Rainier National Park
phone: (206) 569-2211

North Cascades National Park
phone: (206) 856-5700

Olympic National Park
phone: (206) 452-4501

Associations, Publications, etc.

Washington Outfitters & Guides Association
23836 SE 124th Street
Issaquah, WA 98029
phone: (425) 392-6107

Paddle Trails Canoe Club
8909 27th Ave. NE
Seattle, WA 98115

Washington Kayak Club
3048 62nd Ave. SW
Seattle, WA 98116
phone: (206) 933-1178

Washington Bass Federation
President: Jim Owens
16569 - 162nd Place SE
Renton, WA 98058
phone: (425) 271-6569
http://www.wabass.org

DownStream River Runners, Inc.

Casey and Karen Garland

13414 Chain Lake Rd. • Monroe, WA 98272
phone: (360) 805-9899
email: casey@riverpeople.com • www.riverpeople.com

We offer a wide variety of rafting adventures, from tranquil family floats to challenging whitewater descents. We primarily offer one-day trips in Washington, but conduct multiple-day adventures in Oregon as well.

We have been in the business of operating raft trips for 25 years with a perfect safety record. You can be sure that your guides are all experts.

We are state-licensed, insured, and every guide is a nationally certified Swiftwater Rescue Technician.

We raft March through September and have group, family and corporate rates. The rafts are self-bailing and the equipment is state-of-the-art, including wetsuits and boots, which are provided at no additional charge. Reservations are required.

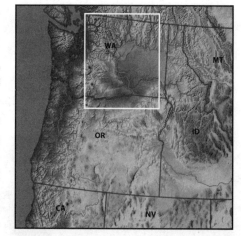

"Thanks to your whole crew for a great day on the Skagit. Your mastery of logistics and ability to organize our large group was a wonder to behold...you are a class act." Ed Smith

SEASONS OF OPERATION

BOAT TYPES

ACTIVITIES

LOCATIONS & SERVICES

Redline River Adventures

Jerry Reddell

24820 Clear Creek Rd. • Darrington, WA 98241
phone: (800) 290-4500 • (360) 436-0284
email: redline@nwoutdoor.com • http://nwoutdoor.com/redline/redline.htm

Redline River Adventures offers a unique rafting experience. Our emphasis is on providing quality river excursions to a wide variety of individuals and groups of all sizes.

We realize that different people seek different levels of intensity in river travel. From heart-pumping whitewater thrills to calm scenic floats, Redline River Adventures has a river trip to suit your needs.

Whether you prefer a one-day excursion or a multi-day camping trip, we allow our guests to enjoy an adventure at their own pace — unhurried and relaxed.

Redline River Adventures offers full- or half-day river excursions on five rivers in the Pacific Northwest. Trips are available from April 1 through September 30, and December 1 through February 15.

"My experience was truly wonderful as it was a birthday gift from my granddaughter to celebrate my 83rd & it is an experience I'll never forget!" Helen P. Burt

SEASONS OF OPERATION

BOAT TYPES

ACTIVITIES

LOCATIONS & SERVICES

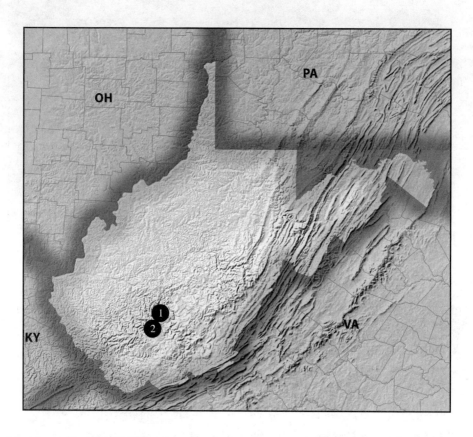

Outdoor Professionals

1 Mountain River Tours, Inc.
2 Wildwater Expeditions Unlimited

License and Report Requirements

• State requires licensing of Outdoor Professionals.

• State requires that Commercial Whitewater Guides file a "Monthly Report of Customers".

Useful information for the state of

West Virginia

State and Federal Agencies

Dept. of Natural Resources
1900 Kanawha Blvd. East
State Building 3
Charleston, WV 25305
Fisheries: (304) 558-2771
Law Enforcement: (304) 558-2771

Forest Service
Eastern Region
310 West Wisconsin Avenue, Room 500
Milwaukee, WI 53203
phone: (414) 297-3646
TTY: (414) 297-3507

Monongahela National Forest
USDA Building
200 Sycamore Street
Elkins, WV 26241-3962
phone/TTY: (304) 636-1800

Bureau of Land Management
Eastern States
7450 Boston Boulevard
Springfield, VA 22153
phone: (703) 440-1600
or (703) 440- Plus Extension
fax: (703) 440-1599

Office Hours: 8:00 a.m. - 4:30 p.m.

Eastern States
Milwaukee District Office
310 W. Wisconsin Ave., Suite 450
(P.O. Box 631 53201-0631)
Milwaukee, WI 53203
phone: (414) 297-4450
fax: (414) 297-4409

Associations, Publications, etc.

Walley World Whitewater Club, West Virginia
http://personal.cfw.com/~bishops/pages/
index.html

American Fisheries Society
PO Box 1278
Elkins, WV 26241
phone: (304) 636-6586
fax: (304) 636-7824

Trout Unlimited West Virginia Council
637 Grand Street
Morgantown, WV 26505-6911
phone: (304) 293-7749

Federation of Fly Fishers
http://www.fedflyfishers.org

West Virginia Bass Chapter Federation
President: John Burdette
25 West Main Street
Buckhannon, WV 26201
phone: (304) 472-3600 or 472-6221

The American Bass Association of
West Virginia
2620 Fairmont Ave., Ste. 110
Fairmont, WV 26554
phone: (304) 366-8183

Mountain River Tours, Inc.

Michael Gray

P.O. Box 88 • Hico, WV 25854
phone: (800) 822-1386 • fax: (304) 658-5817
email: rapidfun@aol.com • http://wvweb.com/www/rapid_fun

Our 27th year!

We offer four- to five-day family "mini-vacations" to wild Class V-plus whitewater on the New and Gauley Rivers in West Virginia.

We have "Express," full-day, and multi-day rafting trips. Mountain biking, rock climbing and hiking adventure packages within the New River Gorge National River and Gauley River National Recreation Area are available.

Mountain River Tours, Inc. also features professional corporate team facilitation and senior float tours.

Enjoy our frequent rafter card: earn points for a free raft trip, youth discounts, campground and deluxe cabins.

"Because of our experiences, my son & I are hooked on whitewater rafting. I feel our experience with Mountain River Tours definitely helped to win us over to rafting!" Patrick McCarty

SEASONS OF OPERATION

BOAT TYPES

ACTIVITIES

LOCATIONS & SERVICES

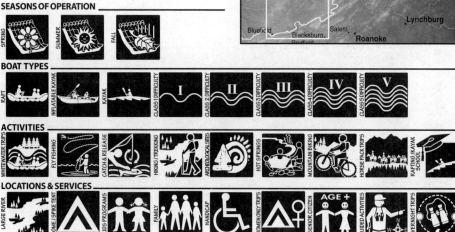

160

Wildwater Expeditions Unlimited

K. Chris Dragan

P.O. Box 155 • Lansing, WV 25862
phone: (800) 982-7238 • (304) 658-4007 • fax: (304) 658-4008
email: wvaraft@wvaraft.com • www.wvaraft.com

Wildwater Expeditions, West Virginia's premier outfitter, is dedicated to a future built upon our proud past. Since 1968, we've been the doorway to the Appalachian Mountains and the timeless beauty and thrilling whitewater found within them. With trips running on the New River and Gualey River, there is a wide range of difficulty levels available to choose from. Come learn the true meaning of "quality time" with your family and friends on a rafting trip. In addition to phenomenal rafting trips, Wildwater Expeditions also offers instructional clinics in kayaking, climbing, and rappelling. All courses are designed around the skill levels of the participants making it possible for you to learn these crafts at a comfortable pace. Hiking, biking, and horseback riding options are also available in the area.

Give Wildwater Expeditions a call to find out why we are still First... on America's Best Whitewater.

"30th year season I was able to make another trip and I'm proud to say that they're as good as ever. Wildwater was the first transit system on the New River, and they're only getting better with age!"
Donald McSorley, Port Washington, NY

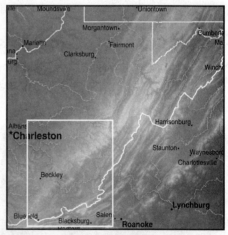

SEASONS OF OPERATION

BOAT TYPES

ACTIVITIES

LOCATIONS & SERVICES

162

Wildwater Expeditions Unlimited

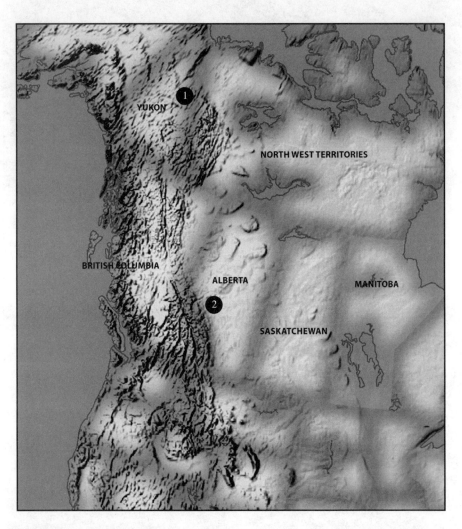

Outdoor Professionals

1 Canoe North Adventures
2 Nahanni Wilderness Adventures

Canada

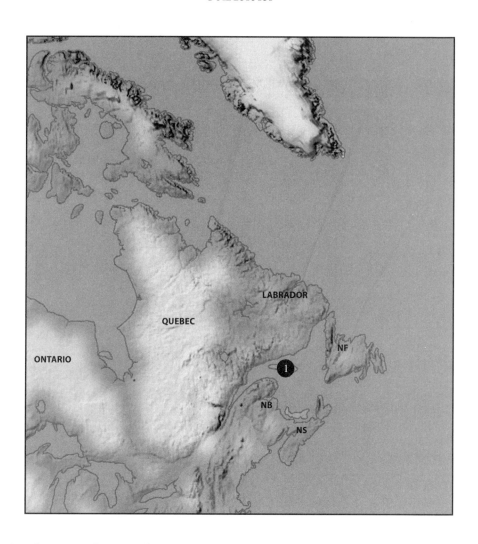

Outdoor Professionals

1 Outside Expeditions

Useful information for the provinces of

Canada

Newfoundland:
Ministries and Agencies

Department of Fisheries & Oceans
200 Kent Street
Ottawa, Ontario Canada K1A 036
phone: (613) 993-0999

Department of Natural Resources
PO Box 8700
St. John's, NF Canada A1B 4J6
phone: (709) 729-4715

Wildlife Division
PO Box 8700
St. John's, NF Canada A1B 4J6
phone: (709) 729-2817

Newfoundland Labrador Wildlife Fed.
phone: (709) 364-8415

Department of Tourism, Culture
& Recreation
PO Box 8730
St. John's, NF, Canada A1B 4J6
phone: (709) 729-2830
fax: (709) 729-1965
email: info@tourism.gov.nf.ca

Associations, Publications, etc.

Federation of Fly Fishers
http://www.fedflyfishers.org

License & Report Requirements

• All outfitters, guides and charter boats
must be registered with each province.

Northwest Territories:

Ministries and Agencies

Department of Resources, Wildlife &
Economic Development

Government of the NW Territories
Scotia Centre, Box 21
600 5102 - 50 Avenue
Yellowknife, N.T. Canada X1A 3S8
phone: (403) 669-2366
fax: (403) 873-0169

License & Report Requirements
• All outfitters, guides and charter boats
must be registered with each province.

Nova Scotia:

Ministries and Agencies

Department of Natural Resources
Western Regional Office
99 High Street
Bridgewater, Nova Scotia, Canada B4V 1V8
phone: (902) 543-0624

Nova Scotia Sports Fisheries
PO Box 700
Pictou, Nova Scotia, Canada B0K 1H0
phone: (902) 485-7022

Department of Fisheries and Oceans
PO Box 1035
Dartmouth, Nova Scotia, Canada 2BY 4T3
phone: (902) 426-9966
toll free in Canada: (800) 565-1633

Nova Scotia Wildlife Disivion
Provincial Building
136 Exhibition Street
Kentville, Nova Scotia, Canada B4N 4E5
phone: (902) 679-6091

License & Report Requirements
• All outfitters, guides and charter boats
must be registered with each province.
• No other reports or licenses needed.

Canada

Ontario:

Ministries and Agencies

Ministry of Natural Resources
Toronto, Ontario, Canada M7A 1W3
phone: (416) 314-2301

Associations, Publications, etc.

The Ontario Federation of Anglers and
Hunters, Inc.
4601 Guthrie Drive, Box 2800
Peterborough, Ont., Canada K9J 8L5
phone: (705) 748-6324
fax: (705) 748-9577
email: ofah@oncomdis

Northern Ontario Tourist Outfitters
Association
269 Main St. West, Suite 408
North Bay, Ontario, Canada P1B 2T8
phone: (705) 748-6324
fax: (705) 748-9577
email: noto@onlink.net
http://virtualnorth.com/noto/

License & Report Requirements

• Need business license to hunt or fish.
  Does not require a year-end report.

• Charter boats/guides are licensed by each
  province.

Prince Edward Island:

Ministries and Agencies

Department of Technology and
Environment
PO Box 2000
Charlottetown, Prince Edward Island
Canada C1A 7N8
phone: (902) 368-4683

Department of Fisheries and Tourism
56 Watts Avenue
Provincial Park, Prince Edward Island
Canada C1E 2B7
phone: (902) 368-4404

License & Report Requirements

• All outfitters, guides and charter boats
  must be registered with each province.
• No reports or licenses needed.

Yukon Territories:

Ministries and Agencies

Dept. of Renewable Resources
Box 2703
Whitehorse, Y.T. Canada 71A 2C6
phone: (403) 667-5460

Associations, Publications, etc.

Yukon Fish & Game Association
PO Box 4434
Whitehorse, Y.T. Canada Y1A 3T5
phone: (403) 667-2843

Yukon Outfitters Association
Box 4548
Whitehorse, Y.T. Canada Y1A 2R8
phone: (403) 668-4118

License & Report Requirements

• All outfitters, guides and charter boats
  must be registered with each province.

Canoe North Adventures

Al Pace and Lin Ward

RR#1, Orangeville • Ontario, Canada L9W 2Y8
phone: (519) 941-6654 • fax: (519) 941-4503

Canoe North offers spectacular wilderness canoe expeditions in Canada's Yukon and Northwest Territories. Guides Al Pace and Lin Ward take pride in building compatible groups of ten trippers with matching skill levels to ensure solid group dynamics.

No-trace camping skills and whitewater paddling strokes are taught to ensure maximum safety and a genuine respect for the remote wilderness regions traveled. Each trip provides personal time for wildlife photography, writing, hiking, and world-class fly fishing.

Wildlife viewing includes moose, caribou, muskox, grizzly and black bear, wolves, fox, sheep, eagles, falcons, cranes and geese. Our top-quality camping gear and hearty gourmet camp meals combined with twenty years of guiding experience ensure that your wilderness adventure will be unforgettable!

"My trip last summer on the Snake River was superbly coordinated by Canoe North Adventures. Al Pace and his wife Lin brought together a tremendous group of ten for the trip and the entire experience was unforgettable." Nick Lewis

SEASONS OF OPERATION

BOAT TYPES

ACTIVITIES

LOCATIONS & SERVICES

Nahanni Wilderness Adventures

David and Wendy Hibbard

Box 4, Site 6 R.R.1 • Didsbury, Alberta, Canada T0M 0W0
phone: (888) 897-5223 • phone/fax: (403) 637-3843
email: adventures@nahanniwild.com • www.nahanniwild.com

Flowing from the heart of the MacKenzie Mountains in Canada's Northwest Territories, the South Nahanni River is steeped in legend and unsurpassed in natural beauty. Its reputation as a pristine and spectacular wilderness river has earned it recognition the world over. Affectionately called Canada's River of Gold, the Nahanni offers its travelers an abundance of natural treasures. The fresh alpine meadows and soaring peaks of the upper river, the thundering cataract of Virginia Falls, the awesome canyons and abundant wildlife make the Nahanni region a kaleidoscope of natural beauty, virtually untouched by people.

Legendary prospectors were lured to the Nahanni seeking their fortune in gold, but it eluded them.

We guarantee you will return home with a wealth of photographs and unforgettable memories.

"A rare and memorable experience for my 50th birthday." Doug Christie

SEASONS OF OPERATION

BOAT TYPES

ACTIVITIES

LOCATIONS & SERVICES

Outside Expeditions

Bryon Howard and Shirley Wright

P.O. Box 337 • North Rustico, Prince Edward Island, Canada C0A 1X0
phone: (800) 207-3899 • (902) 963-3366 • fax: (902) 963-3322
email: info@getoutside.com • www.getoutside.com

Luxury, active vacations featuring extraordinary bicycling tours, sea kayaking, scenic walking tours, wildlife viewing, and much more! All vacations feature first class B & B, hotel, or camping accommodations and premium dining. Enjoy warm waters, catered comfort, and exceptional camping or Inn-to-Inn kayaking, biking, and walking expeditions on Prince Edward Island and Madeleine Island. Although activity is the focus, you rarely paddle, bike, or walk for more than 3 or 4 hours each day, allowing plenty of time for exploring, beach combing, or just relaxing on beaches, or in one of our fine Inn's. Outside Expeditions Coastlines and Country Inns Expedition is soft adventure at its best: warm, safe waters; pastoral scenery and accessible sea animals; with emphasis on great food and beautiful accommodations.

Safe, experienced, fun-loving naturalist guides, delicious meals and memories are around every corner. Beginners welcome.

"Our guides went above & beyond the call of duty to guarantee our complete satisfaction. Everything seemed so lavish..."
Ruth & Matt Colonell, San Luis Obispo, CA

SEASONS OF OPERATION

BOAT TYPES

ACTIVITIES

LOCATIONS & SERVICES

Appendix
&
Questionnaire
&
Indexes

APPENDIX

This is the compete list of the River Guides and Outfitters we contacted during the compilation of our book.

We invited them to participate in our survey by simply sending us their complete client list.

Some replied prizing our idea, but still decided not to participate in our survey. Their main concern was the confidentiality of their client list. We truly respect this position, but we hope to have proven our honest and serious effort. We are sure they will join us in the next edition.

Others participated by sending their client list, but did not qualify for publication. In some cases because of a low score, and in other instances because of an insufficient number of questionnaires returned by their clients.

The names of the outdoor professionals who have qualified by receiving an A rating from their past clients are **bolded** in the Appendix.

United States

Alabama

Company Bass Guide Service
Contact Burch Gray & T.C. Nettles
City Valhermosa Springs
Company Cedar Ridge Hunting Lodge
Contact Fraser Rudd
City Five Point
Company Wheeler Lake Fishing Guides
Contact T.C. Nettles
City Decatur

Alaska

Company Alaska Bound Adventures
Contact George Wagner
City Homer
Company Alaska Discovery
Contact Ken Leghorn & Susan Warner
City Juneau
Company Alaska Mountain & River Adventures
Contact
City Anchorage
Company Alaska Wall Tent Adventures
Contact Ken Manning
City Girdwood
Company Alaska Wildland
Contact Frederick Telleen
City Cooper Landing
Company Alaska's Magnum Outfitters
Contact Keith L. Mattison
City Anchorage
Company Alaskan Outdoor Adventures
Contact John R. Runkle
City Nikolai
Company Alexander Charters
Contact Ron & Michele Alexander
City Ninilchik
Company Anvik River Lodge

Contact Clifford & Cheryl Hickson
City Bethel
Company Beyond Boundaries Expd/ Baranof Wilderness Lodge
Contact Mike Trotter
City Sitka
Company Blue Bayou Charters
Contact John & Dale Mize, Jr.
City Fairbanks
Company Cook Inlet Charters
Contact Bruce & Charlene McLean
City Ninilchik
Company Dan's Alaskan Sportfishing Ventures
Contact Dan Dube
City Anchorage
Company Denali Raft Adventures
Contact Valerie Martin
City Denali Park
Company Fish On with Gary Kernan
Contact Gary Kernan and David Madden
City Kenai
Company Fishing & Hunting Alaska Style
Contact Jeffrey & Vicki Pyska
City Wasilla
Company Flywater Adventures
Contact Richard Culver
City Juneau
Company Glacier Angler Charters
Contact Darrel Shreve
City Valdez
Company Glacier Bay Sea Kayaks
Contact Kara Berg
City Gustavus
Company Hawkeye Adventures
Contact Joseph A. Cross
City Dillingham
Company Hot Rods Guide Service
Contact David Dykstra
City Kasilof
Company J & J Smart Charters
Contact John & Joan Smart
City Chugiak
Company Jiggy's Charters
Contact Eric Lane Lewis
City Petersburg
Company King Salmon Guides, Inc.

Contact Chris Mutert
City King Salmon
Company Kodiak Adventures
Contact Rocky Morgan
City Seward
Company Kodiak Island River Camps
Contact Daniel & Randy Busch
City Kodiak
Company Leonard's Last Frontier Fishing Adv.
Contact Julie & Leonard Ball
City Soldotna
Company Midnight Sun River Runners
Contact Donald Beverlin
City Anchorage
Company Ninilchik Charters
Contact Mike Flores
City Anchorage
Company NOVA
Contact Chuck Spaulding
City Chickaloon
Company Nunivak Island Experiences
Contact Abraham David
City Mekoryuk
Company Nushagak Outfitters
Contact Randy & Adarlene Triplett
City Dillingham
Company Salmon Run Lodge
Contact Janice Balluta
City Nondalton
Company Sea Hook Guides and Charters
Contact Larry Hooton
City Juneau
Company Spirit of Alaska Wilderness Adventures
Contact Steel Davis
City Kodiak
Company Steve's Salmon Charters
Contact Steve Volz
City Yakutat
Company Talaheim Lodge
Contact Mark & Judi Miller
City Anchorage
Company Talstar Lodge
Contact Claire Dubin
City Wasilla
Company The Bush Pilot Inc.

Contact David Scott Haeg
City Soldotna
Company The Charter Company
Contact Jose Polanco
City Anchorage
Company Three Sons Charters
Contact Michael F. Amberg
City Kodiak
Company Tim Berg's Alaskan Fishing Adventures
Contact Timothy Berg
City Soldotna
Company Tokosha Mtn. Lodge
Contact John Neill
City Trapper Creek
Company Trophy Catch Charters
Contact David & Jim Booth Bill
City Palmer
Company Wood River Expeditions
Contact Mark E. Chambers
City Fairbanks
Company
Contact George Siavelis
City Aniak

Arizona

Company Adventure/Discovery Tours
Contact Jene Vredevoogd
City Flagstaff
Company ARA - Wilderness River Adv., Inc.
Contact
City Page
Company Aravaipi Outfitters
Contact Floyd L. Krank
City Globe
Company Arizona Raft Adventures, Inc.
Contact Rob Elliott
City Flagstaff
Company Arizona River Adventues, Inc.
Contact Max Wilson
City Tucson
Company Arizona River Runners, Inc.
Contact Bruce Winter
City Phoenix
Company Bechtel's Big Game Outdoors
Contact Robin W. Bechtel
City Gilbert
Company Canyon Explorations, Inc.
Contact Laurie Staveley
City Flagstaff
Company Canyon R.E.O.
Contact Donnie Dove
City Flagstaff
Company Canyoneers, Inc.
Contact Gaylord Staveley
City Flagstaff
Company Desert Outfitters
Contact Stan T. Graf
City Pearce
Company Desert Voyagers/Rio Grande Rapid Transit
Contact Marsha Blumm

City Scottsdale
Company Diamond River Adventures, Inc.
Contact Les Hibbert
City Page
Company Expeditions, Inc.
Contact Dick McCallum
City Flagstaff
Company Flying E Ranch
Contact
City Wickenburg
Company Grand Canyon Dories/OARS
Contact George Wendt - owner
City Angels Camp, California
Company Horseshoe Ranch
Contact Fred Valentine
City Mayer
Company Hualapai River Runners
Contact
City Peach Springs
Company Outdoors Unlimited
Contact John Vail
City Flagstaff
Company Sprucedale Guest Ranch
Contact Emer & Esther Wiltbank
City Eagar
Company Sun Country Rafting, Inc.
Contact Scott Seyler
City Phoenix
Company Tex Az Wilderness Outfitters
Contact Larry Joe Moore
City Alpine
Company White Stallion Ranch
Contact Russell True
City Tucson
Company Wilderness River Adventures/ Aramark
Contact Stacy Woodward
City Page
Company
Contact Warner D. Glenn
City Douglas

Arkansas

Company Arrowhead Cabin & Canoe Rentals
Contact John Carter
City Caddo Gap
Company Beach Club BBQ & Canoe Rental
Contact
City Hardy
Company Berly
Contact
City Ozark
Company Binks Guide Service
Contact Darrel Binkley
City Norfork
Company Buffalo Adventures Canoe Rental
Contact
City Jasper
Company Buffalo Camping & Canoeing

Contact
City Gilbert
Company Buffalo Outdoor Center
Contact Mike Mills
City Ponca
Company Buffalo Outdoor Center, Silver Hill
Contact
City St. Joe
Company Bull Shoals White River Landing
Contact
City Bull Shoals
Company Carl Phillips Guide Service
Contact Carl E. Phillips
City Yellville
Company Cecil Chism
Contact Cecil Chism
City Norfork
Company Cossatot Outfitters
Contact
City Lockesburg
Company Dirst Canoe Rental
Contact
City Yellville
Company Dodd's Canoe & Jonboat Rental
Contact Julia Dodd
City Yellville
Company Gaston's White River Resort
Contact
City Lakeview
Company Gunga-La Lodge & River Outfitters
Contact
City Lakeview
Company Hamilton Guide Service
Contact Hugh D. Hamilton
City Garfield
Company Kruse's Guide Service
Contact Kenneth F. Kruse
City Fairfield Bay
Company Lindsey's Rainbow Resort
Contact Jared W. Lindsey
City Heber Springs
Company Lobo Landing
Contact
City Heber Springs
Company Miller's Float Service
Contact
City Cotter
Company Newland's Float Trips & Lodge
Contact
City Lakeview
Company North Cadron Canoe Rental
Contact
City Greenbrier
Company Ouachita & Rocky Shoals Canoe Rental
Contact
City Mount Ida
Company Ouachita Joe's Canoe Rental
Contact
City Pencil Bluff
Company Rainbow Drive Resort
Contact
City Cotter
Company Razorback Wilderness Center

Contact
City Dogpatch
Company Red Bud Dock
Contact
City Gassville
Company Red River Trout Dock
Contact Jim Grogan
City Heber Springs
Company River Ranch Resort
Contact
City Heber Springs
Company Riverview Resort
Contact Virgil Bleeker
City Eureka Springs
Company Roundhouse Fly Shop
Contact Todd G. Byers
City Bull Shoals
Company Southfork Canoe Resort
Contact Rick Markway
City Mammoth Spring
Company Sportsman's Resort
Contact Richard Bump
City Flippin
Company Stetson's Resort
Contact
City Flippin
Company Swinging Bridge Resort
Contact
City Heber Springs
Company White Hole Resort
Contact
City Flippin
Company White-Buffalo Resort
Contact
City Mountain Home
Company Woody's Canoe Rental &
Campground
Contact
City Dalton
Company Wright Way Canoe Rental
Contact
City Glenwood
Company
Contact Paul A. Blalock
City Bull Shoals
Company
Contact Burke E. Coles
City Heber Springs
Company
Contact Ronald W. Crawford
City Rogers
Company
Contact James L. Harbour
City Viola
Company
Contact Douglas G. Olson
City Russellville
Company
Contact Max Ramer
City Cotton Plant
Company
Contact Udell E. Schrolder
City Casscoe
Company
Contact Robert Snyder
City Norfork

California

Company A Whitewater Connection
Contact Jim Plimpton
City Coloma
Company Able Whitewater
Contact
City Coloma
Company Access to Adventure
Contact
City Somes Bar
Company Adrift Adventures
Contact Robin Tierney
City Half Moon Bay
Company Adventure Connection, Inc.
Contact Nate Rangel
City Coloma
Company Adventure Rents
Contact Jan Harris
City Gualala
Company Adventure Tours
Contact
City Chico
Company Ahwahnee Whitewater
Contact Jim Gado
City Columbia
Company Alaska Outdoor Adventures
Contact Vito Lopez
City Oroville
Company All Outdoors Adventure
Contact Gregg Armstrong
City Walnut Creek
Company All-Outdoors Adventure Trips
Contact George Armstrong
City Walnut Creek
Company American River Raft Rentals
Contact
City Rancho Cordova
Company American River Recreation
Contact Don Hill
City Lotus
Company American River Touring Assn.
Contact Steve Welch - Mgr
City Groveland
Company American Whitewater
Expeditions
Contact Jon Osgood
City Sunland
Company Arrow Five Outfitters
Contact Tina M. Piazza
City Zenia
Company Aurora River Adventures
Contact
City Willow Creek
Company Banana Boat Riders
Contact
City Avalon
Company Beyond Limits Adventures
Contact Mike Doyle
City Riverbank
Company Bigfoot Rafting Company

Contact
City Willow Creek
Company Blue Waters Kayaking
Contact Kate McClain
City Inverness
Company Burrows Ranch Hunting Club
Contact Bill Burrows
City Red Bluff
Company Chili Bar Outdoor Center
Contact Corky Collier
City Coloma
Company Christian Adventures
Contact Douglas C. Haisch
City Anderson
Company Chuck Richards Whitewater
Contact Chuck Richards
City Lake Isabella
Company Circle H H Hunting Preserve
Contact Fred Hymes
City Nipton
Company Coastal Kayak Fishing
Contact Dennis D. Spike
City Reseda
Company Coloma Country Inn
Contact
City Coloma
Company Danmar Guide Service
Contact Danny J. Redding
City Chico
Company Diamond D Outfitters
Contact Joe S. De Luca
City Weed
Company Echo: The Wilderness Co.
Contact Brad Lord/Dick Linford
City Oakland
Company Echo: The Wilderness
Company
Contact Richard D. Linford
City Oakland
Company Folkestad Fishing Guide
Service
Contact Michael T. Folkestad
City Mission Viejo
Company Friends of the River
Contact
City Sacramento
Company Grand Canyon Dories/OARS
Contact George Wendt - owner
City Angels Camp
Company Gregg Smith Guide Service
Contact Gregg T. Smith
City Redding
Company Hank Mautz Professional
Guide Service
Contact Hank Mautz
City Anderson
Company High Sierra Goat Packing
Contact Claudia Carlson
City Columbia
Company Horse Corral Pack Station
Contact Gayle D. Jones & Nancy Jones
City Midpines
Company IRIE Rafting Company
Contact Amy & Frank E. Wohlfahrt
City Olympic Valley
Company James Henry River Journeys
Contact James H. Katz
City Bolinas

Company JMJ Guide Service
Contact Jeff Gonzales
City Chico
Company Kings River Expeditions
Contact Justin Butchert
City Fresno
Company Klamath River Outfitters
Contact Edna & Wally Watson
City Somes Bar
Company Koksetna Wilderness Lodge
Contact Jonathan H. & Juliann W. Cheney
City Colusa
Company Living Waters Recreation
Contact Tom Harris
City Mt. Shasta
Company Mariah Wilderness Expedition
Contact Donna Hunter
City Point Richmond
Company Michael Coopman's Guide Service
Contact Michael M. Coopman
City Crescent City
Company Mother Lode River Trips
Contact Joe Tassinari
City Coloma
Company Mountain & River Adventures
Contact John Stallone
City Kernville
Company Mountain Travel/Sobek
Contact Perry Robertson
City ElCerrito
Company O.A.R.S., Inc.
Contact George Wendt
City Angels Camp
Company OARS-Outdoor Adventure River Specialists
Contact Eric Grathwol
City Angels Camp
Company Oars, Inc.
Contact Lawrence H. Stettner
City Berkeley
Company Old Indian Guide Fishing Trip
Contact Roy Sanders
City Atwater
Company Outdoor Adventures, Inc.
Contact Robert J. Volpert
City Point Reyes Station
Company Outdoor Recreation/Presidio of Monterey
Contact Terry Siegrist
City Presidio of Monterey
Company R & D Guide Service
Contact James Arden
City Yuba City
Company Redwood Empire Outdoor Adventures
Contact Kenneth D. Bowman
City Miranda
Company River Dancers
Contact John F. McDermott
City Mt. Shasta
Company River Journey
Contact
City Oakdale
Company River Mountain Action
Contact
City Los Angeles

Company River Runners California
Contact
City Calabasas
Company River Travel Center
Contact Annie Nelson, Prudence Parker Raven Earlygrow
City Point Arena
Company Rubicon Whitewater Adventures
Contact
City Forestville
Company S & S Brewer Fishing Service
Contact Stacy Brewer
City Los Molinos
Company Salmon River Outfitters
Contact
City Arnold
Company Sierra Mac River Trips
Contact Marty McDonnell
City Sonora
Company Sierra South Mountain Sports
Contact Tom Moore
City Kernville
Company Southwind Kayak Center, Inc.
Contact Doug Schwartz and Joanne Turner
City Irvine
Company Tahoe Whitewater Tours
Contact Mike Miltner
City Tahoe City
Company The Best of New Zealand Fly Fishing
Contact Mike McClelland
City Santa Monica
Company Tributary Whitewater Tours
Contact Lorraine Hall/Dan Buckley
City Grass Valley
Company Trinity River Rafting
Contact
City Big Bar
Company Turtle River Rafting Company
Contact
City Mt. Shasta
Company Turtle River Rafting Company
Contact Rick Demarest
City Mt. Shasta
Company Waterfall Resort
Contact Monique Littlejohn
City Santa Barbara
Company White Magic Unlimited
Contact Jack Morison
City Mill Valley
Company Whitewater Connection
Contact James M. Plimpton
City Coloma
Company Whitewater Excitement
Contact Norm Schoenhoff
City Auburn
Company Whitewater Expeditions & Tours
Contact
City Sacramento
Company Whitewater Voyages
Contact Bill McGinnis
City El Sobrante
Company Wilderness Adventures
Contact Vickie Irwin
City Mt. Shasta

Company Zephyr River Expeditions
Contact Bob Ferguson
City Columbia
Company
Contact Michael D. Berry
City Bakersfield
Company
Contact Jack Bouche
City Blairsden
Company
Contact Michael D. Charlton
City Somes Bar
Company
Contact Bill Lowe
City Antelope
Company
Contact William Seber
City Sanger
Company
Contact Bob Willogby
City Redding

Colorado

Company A Wanderlust Adventure
Contact Patrick Legel
City Fort Collins
Company Adventure Bound Inc.,River Exp.
Contact Tom & Robin Kleinschnitz
City Grand Junction
Company American Rafting/Lakota River Guides
Contact Darryl Bangert
City Vail
Company Bar Lazy J Guest Ranch
Contact Jerry & Cheri Helmicki
City Parshall
Company Bar X Bar
Contact Clayton Stephenson
City Crawford
Company Bill Dvorak's Kayak and Rafting Expedition
Contact Bill and Jackie Dvorak
City Nathrop
Company Blazing Adventures
Contact Bob Harris
City Snowmass Village
Company Browner's Guide Service
Contact Matt Brown
City Salida
Company Cannibal Outdoors
Contact Jack & Leslie Nichols
City Lake City
Company Chuck Davies Guide Service, Inc.
Contact Chuck & Mark Davies
City Loma
Company Colorado Riff Raft
Contact Peter Hicks
City Aspen
Company Colorado River Runs, Inc.
Contact Joe Kelso
City Bond

Company Colorado Trophy Guides
Contact Jim Stehle
City Commerc City
Company Crampton Mountain Outfitters
Contact Roger Rupp
City Canon City
Company Dawson Guide & Outfitters Service
Contact Douglas & Steven Dawson
City Montrose
Company Durango Rivertrippers
Contact John & Karen Squire
City Durango
Company Four Corners Expeditions, Inc.
Contact Reed K. Dils
City Buena Vista
Company Gafford Outfitters
Contact Jackie Gafford
City Grand Junction
Company High Lonesome Outfitters of Colorado
Contact Mark T. Lumpkins
City Bailey
Company Independent Whitewater
Contact William Block
City Garfield
Company IX7 Cattle Ranch & Outfitter
Contact Chris & Wayne Pond
City Collbran
Company Lazy H Guest Ranch
Contact Karen & Phil Olbert
City Allenspark
Company Lazy Hound Outfitters
Contact Tracey Don Clark - Scott Barnes
City Palisade
Company Lost Valley Ranch
Contact Robert L. Foster
City Sedalia
Company Mild to Wild Rafting
Contact Alex & Molly Mickel
City Durango
Company Mountain Waters Rafting, Inc.
Contact Casey Lynch
City Durango
Company Outward Bound USA
Contact Craig Mackey
City Golden
Company Pagosa Rafting Outfitters
Contact Wayne Walls
City Pagosa Springs
Company Peregrine River Outfitters
Contact Thomas Klema
City Durango
Company Performance Tours, Inc.
Contact Kevin Foley
City Breckenridge
Company Purcell Brothers Outfitting Inc.
Contact Duane & Dale Purcell
City Pueblo
Company Raven Adventure Trips, Inc.
Contact Art Krizman
City Canon City
Company Red Mountain Outfitters
Contact Jim & Mary Flynn
City Alamosa
Company River Runners, Ltd.
Contact David Smith
City Salida

Company Rocky Mountain High Tours Inc.
Contact Dan Davis
City Durango
Company Rocky Mountain Outdoor Center
Contact Alexandra Waldbart
City Howard
Company Rocky Top Outfitters
Contact Steve Packer & Colorado Buck
City Dolores
Company Saddle Mountain Guide Service
Contact Lawrence Zeldenthuis
City Crawford
Company San Juan Outfitting
Contact Tom & Cheri Van Soelen
City Durango
Company Skyline Guest Ranch
Contact Mike & Sheila Farny
City Telluride
Company Small World Adventures
Contact Enga Lokey
City Howard
Company Snowmass Whaitewater, Inc.
Contact Bob Harris
City Snowmass Village
Company Stillwater Gun Club, Inc.
Contact Mark A. Beam
City Brighton
Company Story Creek Outfitters
Contact Frank Menegatti
City Walsenburg
Company Sylvan Dale Ranch
Contact David Jessup and Susan Jessup
City Loveland
Company Telluride Outside
Contact Richard Dudginski
City Telluride
Company Timberwolf Whitewater Expeditions
Contact Larry Meek
City Salida
Company Whitewater Rafting
Contact Ken Larson
City Glenwood Springs
Company Whitewater Voyageurs
Contact John Sells
City Poncha Springs
Company Wilderness Aware Rafting
Contact Joe Greiner
City Buena Vista
Company Woodland Ranch
Contact Elaine & Harry Michael Wood
City Hotchkiss

Connecticut

Company Clarke Outdoors
Contact
City West Cornwall
Company Down River Canoes
Contact
City Haddam

Company Huck Finn Adventures
Contact John Kulick
City Collinsville
Company Main Stream Canoe
Contact
City New Hartford
Company North American Whitewater Expeditions
Contact Elizabeth Mallen & Peter Dostie
City Madison
Company Riverrunning Expeditions
Contact
City Falls Village
Company Small Boat Shop
Contact
City Norwalk
Company The Mountain Workshop
Contact
City Ridgefield
Company White Creek Expeditions
Contact
City New Canaan

Florida

Company Bienville Plantation
Contact Rosemany Townsend
City White Spring
Company Bonnette Hunting & Fishing Club
Contact Alix Bonnette
City Palm Beach Gardens
Company Bounty Hunter Charters 10
Contact Captain Blockhook
City Marathon
Company Capt. Gregory Scott Roe Charters
Contact Gregory Roe, Sr.
City Pt. Charlotte
Company Capt. Jerry A. Williams
Contact
City Tampa
Company Capt. Mike Keech
Contact Sundance Fishing Charters
City Tavernie
Company Catch 22
Contact Capt. Scott Stanczyk
City Islamorada
Company Charlotte Harbor Fishing Charters
Contact Capt. Dan Latham
City Pt. Charlotte
Company Dennis L. Royston
Contact
City Hudson
Company El Rancho Hunting Preserve
Contact Mr. Yates
City Chipley
Company Elbert R. Brown
Contact
City Jupiter
Company Fintastic Charters
Contact Randal J. Eastvold
City Captiva Island

Company Fishing Adventures
Contact Capt. Patrick Gould
City Naples
Company Frank's River Fishing Charter
Service
Contact Frank M. Williams
City Vero Beach
Company Funyet
Contact John Sahagian
City Little Torch Key
Company Happy Hooker One Charters
Contact Captain R.W. Best
City Bradenton
Company No Bones About It
Contact Captain Ann T. Holahan
City Islamorada
Company North American Canoe Tours,
Inc.
Contact Sandee & David Harraden
City Everglades City
Company Taylor Made Sportfishing, Inc.
Contact Jackie Taylor
City Ponce Inlet
Company The Mad Snooker
Contact Captain David J. Pomerleau
City St. Petersburg
Company Thomas L. Mohler
Contact Capt. Tom Mohler
City St. Petersburg
Company Wet Waders
Contact Mark & Mary Emery
City Ocklawaha
Company
Contact Frank E. Bourgeois
City Spring Hill
Company
Contact Capt. Timothy S. Brady
City Everglades City
Company
Contact Bram Broder
City Stuart
Company
Contact Inc. Falcon Charters
City Ft. Lauderdale
Company
Contact Capt. Michael D. Eller
City Destin
Company
Contact George E. Hurst
City Sarasota
Company
Contact Samuel E. O'Briant
City Cape Coral
Company
Contact Capt. Kevin Rosko
City Naples
Company
Contact Mark Sabbides
City Sarasota
Company
Contact Capt. Andy W. Vaughn
City Destin
Company
Contact Capt. William F. Williams
City Lake Worth
Company
Contact Bruce L. & Betty Williams
City Crystal River

Georgia

Company Appalachian Outfitters
Contact
City Dahlonega
Company Mountain Creek Quail Farm
Hunting Pres
Contact Tony Benefield
City Molena
Company Ochlocknee Plantation
Contact Todd Ford
City Sylvester
Company Pretoria Station Hunting
Preserve
Contact John Hayes
City Albany
Company Southeastern Expeditons
Contact Bob Westbrook
City Atlanta
Company Wildewood Outfitters
Contact Anne Gale
City Helen

Hawaii

Company Reel Action Light Tackle
Sportfishing
Contact
City Kailua-Kona
Company Reel Wilderness Adventures,
Inc.
Contact David Taylor
City Mountain View
Company Ulupalakua Hunting Club
Contact Patrick Fisher
City Pukalani

Idaho

Company Aggipah River Trips
Contact Bill & Peggy Bernt
City Salmon
Company Arta River Trips
Contact
City Salmon
Company Barker-Ewing River Trips
Contact
City Salmon
Company Beamer's Landing
Contact F. James & Jill Koch
City Lewiston
Company Bear Valley River Co
Contact Elisabeth Kreipl
City Boise

Company Canyon Cats
Contact Gail Ater-Owner & Roy Akins-Manager
City Riggins
Company Canyons Incorporated
Contact Leslie W. Bechdel
City McCall
Company Cascade Raft & Kayak
Contact Tom Long
City Horseshoe Bend
Company Castaway Fly Shop
Contact Daniel Lee Roope
City Coeur d'Alene
Company Clearwater Outfitters
Contact Leo Crane
City Orofino
Company Clearwater River Company
Contact Jim Cook
City Orofino
Company Cook's Idaho & Wind River
Outfitters
Contact Rick & Judy Cook
City Riggins
Company Diamond Charters
Contact Edwin A. Dickson
City Sandpoint
Company Drury Family
Contact Omer Drury
City Troy
Company Epley's Whitewater
Adventures
Contact Ted & Karen Epley
City McCall
Company Far & Away Adventures
Contact Steve Lentz
City Sun Valley
Company Full Spectrum Tours
Contact
City Sandpoint
Company Headwaters River Company
Contact Betsy Bader & Julie Beppu
City Banks
Company Headwaters River Company,
Inc.
Contact Conrad Fourney
City Banks
Company Henry's Fork Anglers, Inc.
Contact Michael J. Lawson
City Island Park
Company High Adventure River Tours,
Inc.
Contact Randy McBride
City Hagerman
Company Hughes River Expeditions, Inc.
Contact Jerry Hughes
City Cambridge
Company Idaho Afloat
Contact Bruce Howard
City Grangeville
Company Idaho Whitewater Unlimited
Contact Shelly Fisher
City Meridian
Company Lochsa River Outfitters
Contact Sherry Nigard
City Kooskia
Company Mackay Wilderness River Trips,
Inc.
Contact Brent Estep

City Boise
Company Middle Fork River Tours
Contact Kurt & Gayle Selisch
City Hailey
Company Moose Creek Ranch, Inc.
Contact Kelly & Roxanne Van Orden
City Victor
Company Moser's Idaho Adventures
Contact Gary & Paula Moser
City Salmon
Company Moyie River Outfitters
Contact Stanley A. Sweet
City Bonners Ferry
Company Mystic Saddle Ranch
Contact Jeff & Deb Bitton
City Stanley
Company National Outdoor Leadership
School
Contact Benjamin R. Hammond
City Victor
Company Northwest Voyageurs
Contact Jeff Peavey
City Lucile
Company North Fork Store & Cafe
Contact Ken & Dianne Hill
City North Fork
Company R&R Outdoors, Inc.
Contact Robert D. Black
City Pollock
Company R.O.W./River Odysseys West
Contact Peter Grubb & Betsy Bowen
City Coeur d'Alene
Company Rawhide Outfitters
Contact John & Cathy Cranney
City Salmon
Company River Adventures, Ltd.
Contact Sam & Beri Whitten
City Riggins
Company Rocky Mountain River Tours, Inc.
Contact David and Sheila Mills
City Boise
Company S & S Outfitters
Contact David J. Bream
City Lewiston
Company Salmon River Challenge, Inc.
Contact Patrick L. Marek
City Riggins
Company Salmon River Experience
Contact Charles C. Boyd
City Moscow
Company Salmon River Tours Co.
Contact Michael D. McLain
City North Fork
Company Sawtooth Rentals Inc.
Contact
City Stanley
Company Silver Cloud Expeditions
Contact Jerry & Terry Myers
City Salmon
Company Silver Spur Outfitter
Contact Lynn Dalton Tomlison
City DuBois
Company Solitude River Trips
Contact Al & Jeana Bukowsky
City Merlin, Oregon
Company St. Joe Hunting & Fishing
Camp, Inc.

Contact Will & Barbara Judge
City St. Maries
Company Sun Valley Rivers Company, Inc.
Contact Jon Charles & Melanie McGregor
City Sun Valley
Company Tews Ranches
Contact Rusty & Carla Tews
City Shoshone
Company Triangle C Ranches
Contact Ron Gillett
City Stanley
Company Triple O Outfitters, Inc.
Contact D.A. & Barbara Opdahl Harlan
City Pierce
Company Victor Frederickson Outfitter & Guide
Contact Victor Frederickson
City Naples
Company Wally York & Son, Inc.
Contact W. Travis York
City Elk City
Company Wapiti River Guides
Contact Gary Lane
City Riggins
Company Warren River Expeditions, Inc.
Contact David F. Warren
City Salmon
Company Wilderness River Outfitters & Trail Exp.
Contact Joseph Lewis Tonsmeire
City Lemhi
Company Worldwide Outdoor Adventures
Contact Randy Beck
City Lewiston

Illinois

Company Doctorman's Cache Core Hunting Preserve
Contact Dean Doctorman
City Ullin
Company Dyer for Hire Pro Fishing Guide
Contact Joe Dyer
City Stering
Company Rend Lake Conservancy Dist.
Contact Dennis Sneed
City Benton
Company Richmond Hunting Club
Contact Mike Daniels
City Richmond
Company Riverwood Game Preserve, Ltd.
Contact Sam Biswell
City Tennessee
Company Rock River Professional Guide Service
Contact Denny Halgren
City Dixon
Company Sandy Creek Ranch

Contact Steve M. Wheeler
City Winchester
Company Saukenuk Paddlers
Contact
City Moline
Company Tri R Shooting Preserve
Contact R.G. Swearingin
City Jerseyville

Indiana

Company Banzai Charter
Contact Capt. Ralph Miyata
City LaPorte
Company Clements Canoes, Inc.
Contact Greg & Joan Woods
City Crawfordsville
Company Lost River Game Farm
Contact Bob Hudelson
City Orleans
Company Lyon's Shooting Preserve
Contact John Lyons
City Portland
Company Maier Pheasant Farm & Hunting
Contact Josephine Maier
City Bremen

Iowa

Company Backwater Outfitters
Contact
City Clinton
Company Bluffton Canoe Rental & Campground
Contact
City Cresco
Company Canoe Sport Outfitters
Contact Jeff Holmes
City Indianola
Company CanoeSport Outfitters
Contact
City Indianola
Company Dam Bait Shop
Contact
City Linn Grove
Company Deliverance Canoes
Contact
City Bonaparte
Company Ellis Harbor Concession
Contact
City Cedar Rapids
Company Hruska's Canoe Livery
Contact
City Cresco
Company Iowa Sure Shot Guide Service
Contact Randy Risetter
City Fort Dodge
Company J & B Canoe Outfitters

Contact
City Waukon
Company Payne's Canoe Rental
Contact
City Quasqueton
Company Raccoon River Valley Outfitters
Contact
City Adel
Company Thor Hunting Adventures
Contact Tim Burres
City Thor
Company Turkey River Canoe Trips
Contact
City Elkader
Company University of Iowa Kayak & Canoe Club
Contact
City Iowa City

Kansas

Company Broken Bar 7 Hunting Safari
Contact Kaye O'Brien
City Saint Francis
Company Flint Hills Guide Service
Contact Brian L. Wheeler
City Cottonwood Falls
Company Old Indian Guide Service
Contact David R. Warren
City Leon
Company Ole Olson's Wild Bird Hunt
Contact Jeffrey D. Olson
City Lindsborg
Company R M F Guide Service
Contact Ronald M. Ford
City Manhattan
Company Thunder Prairie Guide Service
Contact Timothy R. Larson
City Hartford
Company Wolf River Outfitter
Contact Tony French & Tom Johansen Jim Aller
City Hiawatha

Kentucky

Company Deer Creek Outfitters
Contact Tim Stull
City Sebree
Company Sheltowee Trace Outfitters
Contact Rick Egedi
City Whitley City

Louisiana

Company Capt. Phil Robichaux Saltwater Guide
Contact Phil Robichaux
City Marrero
Company Custom Charters
Contact Captain Tommy Pellegrin
City Houma
Company Fishunter Guide Service Inc.
Contact Nash Roberts III & Nash Roberts IV
City New Orleans
Company Guided Louisiana Woodcock Hunts
Contact Charles L. Sutton
City Ferriday
Company Pin Oak Mallards Lodge
Contact Ace Cullum
City Rayville
Company The Other Coast
Contact Capt. Briant Smith
City Lake Charles

Maine

Company All Outdoors
Contact Larry Totten
City West Bath
Company Attean Camps & Guide Service
Contact Hal & Debbie Blood
City Jackman
Company Buck Stop Sporting Camps
Contact Richard Streeter
City Allagash
Company Camp Wapiti
Contact Anita & Frank Ramelli
City Patten
Company Coastal Maine Outfitters
Contact Joe Lucey, Jr.
City Belfast
Company Crab Apple Whitewater, Inc.
Contact Chuck Peabody
City The Forks
Company Driftwood Lodge
Contact Harold Schmidt
City Shin Pond
Company Gilpatrick's Guide Service
Contact Gil Gilpatrick
City Skowhegan
Company Hallenbeck Guide Service, Inc.
Contact Thomas Hallenbeck
City Brownfield
Company Magic Falls Rafting Co.
Contact David Neddeau
City West Forks
Company Maine Exploratiaons
Contact Bonnie Pooley
City Bethel
Company Maine Whitewater, Inc.
Contact James Ernst
City Bingham
Company Moxie Outdoor Adventures
Contact Cliff Stevens

City West Forks
Company New England Whitewater Center
Contact Matt Polstein
City Millinocket
Company North Country Rivers, Inc.
Contact Jim Murton
City Wassalboro
Company Northern Outdoors, Inc.
Contact Suzanne Hockmeyer
City The Forks
Company Penobscot Canoe Expeditions
Contact Mike Dougherty
City Orono
Company Professional River Runners of Maine
Contact Ed Beauchamp
City W. Forks
Company Ray's Guide Service
Contact Raymond Reitze, Jr.
City Canaan
Company Red's Guide Service
Contact Barbara Pineau
City Aurora
Company River Drivers
Contact Arthur Dresser
City Bath
Company The Chewonki Foundation
Contact Greg Shute
City Wiscasset
Company The Homestead Lodge
Contact Gloria Nelson
City Oxbow
Company Unicorn Rafting Expeditions
Contact Jay Schurman
City Lake Parlin
Company Unicorn Rafting Expeditions, Inc.
Contact
City Brunswick
Company Wheaton's Lodge
Contact
City Forest City
Company Wilderness Adventures
Contact Daniel Pettingill
City Palmyra
Company Wilderness Expeditions, Inc.
Contact John Willard
City Rockwood
Company Women Backcountry Guided Adventure
Contact Dail Marie Martin
City Yarmouth
Company
Contact Brad Rounds
City Cumberland

Maryland

Company AAA Charterboat Captains, Inc.
Contact Captain George A. Prenant
City Deale
Company Chesapeake Expeditions
Contact Capt. Norman Haddaway

City Claiborne
Company Pete's Corvette Fishing Charters
Contact Captain Pete Bowman
City Ocean City
Company Potomac Guide Service
Contact Captain William P. Kremer
City Gaithersburg
Company Precision Rafting of the Gauley, Inc.
Contact Roger Zabel
City Friendsville
Company Quaker Neck Gun Club, Inc.
Contact Tyler Johnson
City Chestertown
Company River & Trail Outfitters
Contact W. Lee Baihly
City Knoxville
Company Sheaffer's Hunting Preserve
Contact Peter Shaeffer
City Centreville
Company Upper Yough Expeditions
Contact Gary Davis
City Friendsville
Company
Contact Michael D. Cassidy
City West River
Company
Contact Capt. Christopher L. Ludlow
City Friendship
Company
Contact Alex D. Williams
City Deale

Massachusetts

Company Berkshire Backcountry
Contact David Carlow
City Adams
Company Come Fly With Me
Contact Captain Chris Jop
City Marion
Company Zoar Outdoor Adventure Resort, Inc.
Contact Bruce Lessels
City Charlemont

Michigan

Company Bachelor One Charters
Contact Willliam B. MacLean
City Holland
Company Captain Steve Paslaski
Contact Captain Steve Paslaski
City Oscoda
Company Cudney's Big Bucks
Contact Joseph E. Cudney
City Copemish
Company King's Charter Service

Contact John E. King
City Manistee
Company MGM Charters
Contact Gary R. Mitzel
City Harrison Twp.
Company Miller's Sport Fishing
Contact Don S. Miller
City Saline
Company NorthBay Charters
Contact Capt. Tom E. Arlington
City New Baltimore
Company Pine Hill Kennel & Sportsmen's Club
Contact James S. Rypkema
City Rockford
Company Rustic Ridge Hunt Club
Contact Michael A. Shoup
City Martin
Company Salmon Nailer Charters
Contact Ora Swick
City Takonsha
Company Sea Witch Charters
Contact Ed Peplinski
City Lake Leelanau
Company Sky High Outfitters of New Mexico
Contact James E. Johnson
City Midland
Company Sports Page Charter
Contact Robert N. Willick
City Alpena
Company Stream Fever
Contact Bob Linsenman
City Rose City
Company The Huntsman Hunt Club, Inc.
Contact James & Nora Tebben
City Dryden
Company Whisky River Hunt Club
Contact Michael A. Damman
City Hillsdale
Company
Contact Dennis Bidigare
City St. Clair Shores
Company
Contact Captain Larry E. Lienczewski
City Bay City
Company
Contact Gordon M. Shovan
City Harrisville

Minnesota

Company Cascade Kayaks
Contact John Amren
City Lutsen
Company Clearwater Lodge & Canoe Outfitters
Contact Marti & Bob Marchino
City Grand Marais
Company Gloege's Northern Sun Canoe Outfitting
Contact
City Sebeka
Company God's Country Outfitters

Contact
City Grand Rapids
Company Hungry Jack Outfitters & Cabins
Contact David & Nancy Seaton
City Grand Marais
Company Huntersville Canoe Outfitters
Contact
City Menahga
Company Irv Funk Canoe Outfitters
Contact
City Sebeka
Company Jack & Toni's Fall Lake Log Cabins
Contact Jack & Toni Dulinsku
City Ely
Company Jackpine Lodge
Contact Don & Connie Stocks
City Ely
Company Ketter Canoeing
Contact Betty Ketter
City Minneapolis
Company Kuduk Guide Service
Contact Chris Kuduk
City Milaca
Company La Croix Outfitters
Contact
City Cook
Company Lac Qui Parle Hunting Camp
Contact Steve
City Montevideo
Company Midwest Mountaineering
Contact
City Minneapolis
Company Minnesota Horse & Hunt Club
Contact
City Prior Lake
Company Mooosehorn Resort
Contact Alan & Miriam Burchell
City Ray
Company North Country Lodge
Contact John Swenson
City Ely
Company Northern Expeditions-High Adventure
Contact Northern Tier National High Adv.
City Ely
Company Northernaire Floating Lodges
Contact Charles & Jane Levene
City International Falls
Company Northwind Lodge
Contact Joe & Paula Baltich
City Ely
Company Rockwood Lodge
Contact Tim Austin
City Grand Marais
Company Sawtooth Outfitters - MN
Contact Derald & Ginny Storlie
City Tofte
Company Seagull Cabins & Canoe Outfitters
Contact Debbie Mark & Roger Hahn
City Grand Marais
Company Steamboat Bay Resort
Contact Sherman & Cynthia Flackus
City Walker
Company Superior Whitewater Rafting

Tours
Contact
City Carlton
Company Taylors Falls Canoe Rental
Contact
City Taylors Falls
Company Terry's Boat Harbor
Contact Terry & Vicky Thurmer
City Garrison
Company Timber Trail Lodge & Outfitters
Contact Bill & Marge Forsberg
City Ely
Company Top of the Trail Outfitters
Contact Jeff Drew
City Grand Marais
Company Tuscarora Lodge & Canoe Outfitters
Contact Jim & Ann Leeds Kerry
City Grand Marais
Company Welch Mill Canoeing & Tubing
Contact
City Welch
Company Wilderness Canoeing
Contact
City Willow River
Company Wilderness Inquiry
Contact Greg Lais
City Minneapolis
Company Wing Shooters Inc., Sedan Hunt Club
Contact Ed Nighbert
City Sedan
Company
Contact Frank E. Nelson
City Big Falls

Mississippi

Company Belmont Shooting Preserve
Contact Shirley Goddard
City Belmont
Company McKenna Ranch
Contact Steve McKenna
City Pachuta
Company Plum Nellie's Mallard Den
Contact Guy Wilson
City Leland
Company Wolf River Canoes, Inc.
Contact
City Long Beach

Missouri

Company Bass' River Resort
Contact
City Steelville
Company Can You Canoe
Contact
City Lebanon

Company Cedar Haven Park
Contact Teresa Rupnig
City Theodosia
Company Circle J Campgrounds
Contact
City Lebanon
Company Clear Fork Hunting Preserve
Contact Ronald & Ruth Dillingham
City Warrensburg
Company Devils Back Floats
Contact Delores Swoboda
City Leslie
Company Expedition Outfitters
Contact Mike Manzo
City North Kansas City
Company Fagan's Meramec River Canoe & Raft
Contact
City Steelville
Company Fletcher's Devil's Dive Resort
Contact
City Eagle Rock
Company Ford's Canoe Rental
Contact
City Cedar Hill
Company G&L's Getaway
Contact
City Lesterville
Company Garrison's Canoe Rental
Contact
City Steelville
Company Gracies Canoe-Camp
Contact
City Pineville
Company Green's Meramec Canoe & Raft Rental
Contact
City Steelville
Company Heflin's Floats
Contact Harry Heflin
City Jerome
Company Hidden Valley Campground
Contact Bill Cheek
City Cascade
Company Ho-Humm Canoe Rental
Contact
City Lebanon
Company Hufstedler's Store & Canoe Rental
Contact
City Alton
Company Indian Springs Lodge Canoe & Raft
Contact
City Steelville
Company J&M Canoe Rental
Contact Diane Newman
City Crane
Company Jacks Fork Canoe Rental
Contact
City Eminence
Company Jadwin Canoe Rental
Contact Darrell Blackwell
City Jadwin
Company Kevin's Canoe & Raft Rental
Contact
City Cuba
Company Light's Floats

Contact
City Jerome
Company Meramec State Park Lodge & Canoe
Contact
City Sullivan
Company Mountain Creek Campground
Contact
City Eldridge
Company Muddy River, Inc.
Contact Robert Hoenike
City Kansas City
Company North Fork River Outfitters
Contact
City Dora
Company OMAO Resort
Contact
City Caulfield
Company Ozark Springs Resort
Contact
City Richland
Company Ozark Sunrise Expeditions, Inc.
Contact
City Joplin
Company Pettit Canoe Rental
Contact
City Caulfield
Company Richards Canoe Rental
Contact
City Alton
Company Sand Spring Resort
Contact
City Lebanon
Company Sho-Me Rental & Rafting
Contact
City Sullivan
Company Steelville Raft Rental
Contact Linda Fagen
City 65565
Company The Hobbie Hut
Contact Vince & Zelda Smith
City Perry
Company The Rafting Co.
Contact
City Steelville
Company Tilson's Tradin Post
Contact
City Tecumseh
Company Vogels Canoe Rental
Contact
City Lebanon
Company Wade's On the Edge Resort
Contact
City Licking
Company Wild River Canoe Rental
Contact
City Salem
Company Windy's Canoe & Tube Rental
Contact Donna Smith
City Eminence
Company Woods' Float & Canoe Rental
Contact
City Alton
Company Yellow Bluff Canoe Rental
Contact
City Dixon

Montana

Company 10,000 Waves, Raft & Kayak Adventures
Contact Deb Moravec
City Missola

Company 63 Ranch
Contact Sandra M. Cahill
City Livingston

Company Absaroka Rafting Adventures
Contact
City Gardiner

Company Absaroka River Adventures
Contact Matt Holtz
City Absarokee

Company Adventure Whitewater
Contact Marek Rosin
City Red Lodge

Company Adventures Big Sky
Contact Patrick Dillon
City Big Sky

Company Alta Meadow Ranch
Contact Britt Litchford
City Darby

Company Anderson's Yellowstone Angler
Contact George R. Anderson
City Livingston

Company Angler's Edge
Contact Paul R. Rice
City Livingston

Company Anglers Afloat, Inc.
Contact David J. O'Dell
City Stevensville

Company Arrick's Fishing Flies
Contact Arrick Lyle Swanson
City West Yellowstone

Company Babcock Creek Outfitters
Contact LeRoy Books
City Kalispell

Company Bad Beaver Bikes, Skis & Tours
Contact Susan Renfro
City Dillon

Company Bar Six Outfitters
Contact Terry D. Throckmorton
City Dillon

Company Barnes Brothers, Inc.
Contact Jack R. Joyce
City Hardin

Company Bear Creek Lodge
Contact Roland & Elizabeth Turney
City Victor

Company Bear's Den Outfitters, Inc.
Contact Bruce C. Delorey
City Livingston

Company Beartooth Whitewater
Contact Randow Parker
City Red Lodge

Company Beaver Creek Outfitters
Contact Clayton A. Barkhoff
City Lewistown

Company Beavertail Outfitters
Contact Dennis Rehse
City Dillon

Company Big Bear Lodge
Contact Scott Sanders
City Cooke City

Company Big Hole River Outfitters

Contact Craig Fellin
City Wise River

Company Bighorn Angler
Contact Scott Steinfeldt & Donald Cooper
City Fort Smith

Company Bighorn River Fin & Feathers
Contact James L. Pickens
City Billings

Company Bighorn River Resorts
Contact Nick C. Forrester
City Hardin

Company Bighorn Trout Shop
Contact Hale C. Harris & Steve Hilbers
City Fort Smith

Company Bill Johnson Outfitters
Contact
City Dillon

Company Birds of Plenty
Contact Curt Olson & Dennis Schaffer
City Broadus

Company Bitterroot Anglers
Contact Andre August Carlson
City Stevensville

Company Black Mountain Outfitters
Contact Scott & Sandy Sallee
City Emigrant

Company Blue Ribbon Fishing Tours
Contact Dale D. Siegle
City Livingston

Company Bob Marshall Wilderness Ranch
Contact
City Seeley Lake

Company Bob's Tackle Box
Contact Bob A. Cleverley
City Ennis

Company Brant Oswald Fly Fishing Service
Contact Brant Konrad Oswald
City Livingston

Company Bud Lilly's Trout Shop
Contact Dick Greene
City West Yellowstone

Company Butler Outfitters
Contact Earl Butler
City Darby

Company Cabinet Mountain Adventures, Inc.
Contact Bill & Ken
City Troy

Company Canoeing House/Blue Ribbon Guide
Contact Allan L. Anderson
City Three Forks

Company Captain Trout Outfitter & Guides
Contact Robert Coppock
City Bozeman

Company Cast and Blast Outfitters
Contact Curt D. Collins
City Billings

Company Chan Welin's Big Timber Fly Fishing
Contact Channing W. Welin
City Big Timber

Company Chico Hot Springs Lodge
Contact Colin Davis

City Pray

Company Cinnamon Lodge
Contact Jim & Joe Snyder
City Gallatin Gateway

Company Circle Bar Guest Ranch
Contact Sarah Stevenson
City Utica

Company Clark's Guide Service
Contact Edward C. Clark
City Ennis

Company Crazy Mountain Raft
Contact Robert H. Wiltshire
City Livingston

Company Curtiss Outfitters
Contact Ronald L. Curtiss
City Kalispell

Company Custom River Outfitters
Contact J. Ellery & T. Patrick Steven Heaverlo
City Helena

Company Dan Bailey's Fly Shop
Contact John P. Bailey
City Livingston

Company Diamond Hitch Outfitters
Contact Chris McNeill
City Dillon

Company Diamond J Ranch
Contact Tim Combs
City Ennis

Company Doonan Gulch Outfitters
Contact Russell E. Greenwood
City Broadus

Company Elk Creek Outfitters
Contact Gerald K. Olson
City Wilsall

Company Espresso Outfitters
Contact
City Hot Springs

Company Five Valleys Flyfishers
Contact Chris E. Nelson
City Missoula

Company Flatline Outfitters
Contact Matthew Greemore
City Emigrant

Company Fly Fishers' Inn
Contact Richard W. Pasquale
City Cascade

Company Fly-Fishing Montana Company
Contact Randall J. Ziegler
City Bozeman

Company Flyfishing Montana & Chile
Contact Michael C. Mosolf
City Dillon

Company Flying D Ranch
Contact Beau Turner Ida Mutchie
City Gallatin Gateway

Company Frontier Anglers
Contact Timothy M. Tollett
City Dillon

Company Ft. Musselshell Outfitters
Contact Bill Harris
City Winnett

Company G Bar M Ranch
Contact
City Clyde Park

Company Geyser Whitewater Expeditions, Inc.
Contact Eric Becker

City Gallatin Gateway
Company Glacier Motorsports, Inc.
Contact Larry Eddy
City Columbia Falls
Company Glacier Raft Co.
Contact Daniel Howlett
City Polson
Company Glacier Sea Kayaking
Contact Bobbie Gilmore
City Whitefish
Company Glacier Wilderness Guides
Contact Cris Gayner
City Whitefish
Company Golden Sedge Drifters
Contact Gregory A. Childress
City Broadus
Company Gone Clear Outfitters
Contact Dave Hall
City Bozeman
Company Great Bear & Landers Fork
Outfitters
Contact H.J. Gilchrist
City Great Falls
Company Great Northern Whitewater,
Inc.
Contact Deedee Baldwin
City West Glacier
Company Great Waters Outfitting
Contact John Keeble & Mark Lane
City Melrose
Company Grizzly Hackle Outfitters
Contact James Edward Toth
City Missoula
Company Harman's Fly Shop
Contact Thomas J. Harman
City Sheridan
Company Hawley Mountain Guest
Ranch
Contact Cathy Johnson
City McLeod
Company Headwaters Guide Service
Contact Robin Cunningham
City Gallatin Gateway
Company Heinecke Outfitting & Guide
Service
Contact William F. Heinecke
City Helena
Company Hell's A Roarin' Outfitters
Contact Warren H. Johnson
City Gardiner
Company High Country Outfitters
Contact Chip Rizzotto
City Pray
Company High Plains Drifter
Contact Mike Hillygus
City Missoula
Company Howard Outfitters
Contact Dale Patrick Howard
City Ennis
Company Howard Zehntner Hunting
Contact Howard Zehntner
City White Sulphur Springs
Company Hubbard's Yellowstone
Outfitter
Contact James L. Hubbard
City Bozeman
Company Jack River Outfitters
Contact Jim Allison

City Ennis
Company Jacklin's Outfitters
Contact Robert V. Jacklin
City West Yellowstone
Company Jerry Crabs Fly Fisher
Contact Jerry Crabs
City Bozeman
Company John Greene's Fly Fishing
Service
Contact John J. Greene
City Livingston
Company John Hanson MTI, Inc.
Contact John Hanson
City Belgrade
Company John Maki Outfitters
Contact John C. Maki
City Helena
Company JR Outfitters
Contact Corky & Clarice Hedrick
City Absarokee
Company LaMarche Creek Outfitting Co.
Contact Russell B. Smith
City Philipsburg
Company Last Best Place Tours
Contact Graeme R. McDougal
City Dillon
Company Lewis & Clark Trail Adventures
Contact Wayne Fairchild
City Missoula
Company Linehan Outfitting Co.
Contact Timothy Linehan
City Troy
Company Lone Tree Fly Goods
Contact David W. Borjas
City Dillon
Company Lone Willow Creek Guide
Service
Contact Jim M. Schell
City Livingston
Company Loons Echo Resort
Contact Ed Hynes
City Stryker
Company Lower Clark Fork River
Outfitters
Contact Donn R. Dale
City St. Regis
Company M & M Outfitters
Contact Monty D. Hankinson
City Dillon
Company Madison River Fishing Co.
Contact Michael D. Pollack
City Ennis
Company Madison Valley Cabins
Contact Gary F. Evans
City Cameron
Company Many Rivers Outfitting
Contact Daniel Guy Miller
City Great Falls
Company Maountain Trail Outfitters
Contact David Gamble
City Livingston
Company Miller Barber's Streamline
Anglers
Contact John Herzer
City Missoula
Company Mission Mountain Outfitters
Contact Richard R. Bishop
City Seeley Lake

Company Missouri River Canoe Co.
Contact
City Loma
Company Missouri River Expeditions
Contact Timothy G. Plaska
City Clancy
Company Missouri River Outfitters, Inc.
Contact Larry Cook
City Fort Benton
Company Montana Adventures in
Angling
Contact James McFadyean
City Billings
Company Montana Blue Ribbon
Outfitters Big Sky
Contact Edward G. Renaud
City Helena
Company Montana River Guides
Contact Gregory G. Mentzer
City Wolf Creek
Company Montana Rivers to Ridges
Contact Daniel J. Pluth
City Big Sky
Company Montana Safaris
Contact Rocky & Lorell Heckman
City Choteau
Company Montana Trout Trappers
Contact Jim Cox
City Missoula
Company Montana Whitewater
Contact Bill Zell
City Bozeman
Company Montana's Master Angler Fly
Service
Contact Thomas M. Travis
City Livingston
Company Montella From Montana
Contact Richard Montella
City Fort Smith
Company Mountain Leisure Trading Co.
Contact Sherman Brown
City Great Falls
Company No Cut Throats Outfitting
Contact Craig A. Clevidence
City Kalispell
Company Northern Llights Outdoor
Center
Contact John Gangemi
City Bigfork
Company Northern Rockies Natural
History
Contact Ken Sinay
City Bozeman
Company Northwest Voyageurs
Contact
City Whitefish
Company Old West Angler & Outfitters
Contact Jim Yeager
City Columbus
Company Outlaw River Runners/Great
Bear
Contact Greg Nelson
City Kalispell
Company Pangaea Expeditions
Contact Karla James
City Missoula
Company Paradise Valley
Contact David R. Handl

City Livingston
Company Parks' Fly Shop
Contact Richard C. Parks
City Gardiner
Company R.J. Cain & Company Outfitters
Contact R.J. Cain
City Ennis
Company Rainbow Chasers
Contact Larry Cawlfield
City Helena
Company Rainbow Guide Service
Contact Joseph Daniel Biner
City Darby
Company Rainbow Outfitters
Contact Jim L. Becker
City Polaris
Company Randy Brown's Madison Flyfisher
Contact Randall W. Brown
City Ennis
Company River Resource Enterprises
Contact Mark Jones
City Missoula
Company Riveride Motel & Outfitters
Contact Robert Hines
City Ennis
Company Rocking W Outfitters
Contact Bill & Billy White
City Darby
Company Rocky Mountain Whitewater
Contact Patrick W. Doty
City East Missoula
Company Royal Outfitters
Contact Tyrone L. Throop
City Hall
Company Running River Fly Guide
Contact Stuart W. Howard
City Bozeman
Company S.W. Montana Fishing Co.
Contact David V. Marsh
City Sheridan
Company Saunders Floating
Contact William C. Saunders
City Ennis
Company Schneider's Guide Service
Contact Kenneth LeRoy Schneider
City St. Xavier
Company Shiplet Ranch Outfitters
Contact Bob & Barbara Shiplet
City Clyde Park
Company Sierra Safaris Wilderness Tours
Contact Carl Swoboda
City Livingston
Company Skalkaho Ldge. Outftr. & Guides
Contact John V. Rose
City Hamilton
Company Slip & Slide Guide Service
Contact Franklin J. Rigler
City Gardiner
Company Stillwaters Outfitting
Contact Lee R. Scherer
City Billings
Company Stockton Outfitters
Contact Billy D. Stockton
City Wise River
Company Sun Canyon Lodge
Contact Lee Carlbom

City Augusta
Company Sun Raven Guide Service
Contact Katherine Howe
City Livingston
Company Sun Trek Outfitters
Contact John J. Humble
City Missoula
Company Swan Valley Llamas
Contact
City Condon
Company Sweetcast Angler
Contact Steve Pauli
City Big Timber
Company Tamarack Lodge
Contact William A. McAfee
City Troy
Company The Fishhook
Contact Dominic "Dee" Carestia
City Wise River
Company The Rising Wolf Ranch
Contact
City East Glacier
Company The River's Edge
Contact David W. Corcoran
City Bozeman
Company The Tackle Shop
Contact Tim Combs
City Ennis
Company Trapper Creek Outfitters
Contact John A. Metz
City Conrad
Company Triple M Outfitters
Contact Mark J. Faroni
City Dixon
Company Trout Fishing Only
Contact William M. Abbot
City Hamilton
Company Troutfitters
Contact Frank M. Stanchfield
City Wise River
Company Trouthawk Outfitters
Contact Randolph R. Scott
City Missoula
Company Troutwest
Contact Thomas J. Laviolette
City Livingston
Company Voyageurs of the Roche Jaune
Contact Tom White
City Billings
Company Wapiti Basin Outfitters
Contact Dan Reddick
City
Company Western Timberline Outfitters
Contact Dawn Krebs
City Plains
Company Western Waters and Woods
Contact Gail Gutsche./Dan Ward/Matt Thomas
City Missoula
Company Wild Rockies Tours
Contact Jerry Nichols
City Missoula
Company Wilderness Outfitters
Contact John Everett Stoltz
City Livingston
Company Williams Guide Service
Contact Don A. Williams
City Livingston

Company Wolf Creek Guide Service
Contact Steve Butts
City Wolf Creek
Company Wolverine Creek Outfitters
Contact Craig Shell
City Cooke City
Company Wolverton Outfitters
Contact Keith Wolverton
City Great Falls
Company WRP Fly Fishing Outfitters
Contact Bill Page
City Livingston
Company Yellowstone Fly Fisher
Contact Mike Sprague
City Livingston
Company Yellowstone Troutfitters
Contact Andy Szofran
City Red Lodge
Company
Contact Daniel E. Glines
City Ennis
Company
Contact LeRoy G. Senter
City Livingston
Company
Contact Doug Swisher
City Hamilton
Company
Contact Dudley L. Tyler
City Big Timber
Company
Contact James K. Tyler
City Big Timber

Nebraska

Company Brewers Canoers & Tubers
Contact Randy & Mary Mercure
City Valentine
Company Fairfield Campgrounds
Contact Beryl Kuhre & Loretta Kuhre Daniels
City Johnstown
Company Graham Canoe Outfitters
Contact Doug & Twyla Graham
City Valentine
Company Hunt Nebraska, Inc.
Contact Johnny Hemelstrand
City Arapahoe
Company Little Outlaw Canoe & Tube Rental
Contact Rich Mercure
City Valentine
Company Rocky Ford Camp & Canoe Base
Contact Alan & Mary Stokes
City Valentine
Company Sharp's Outfitters
Contact
City South Sparks
Company Sunny Brook Camp Outfitters
Contact Roy & Steve Breuklander
City Sparks
Company Supertubes

Contact N. Moosman
City Valentine
Company
Contact Lou & Jan Christiansen
City Sparks

Contact David Showell
City Absecon

City Albuquerque

Nevada

Company Black Canyon Raft Tours
Contact Ron Opfer
City Boulder City
Company Davis Whitewater Expeditions
Contact Lyle Davis
City Winnemucca
Company East Point Kennels & Guiding Service
Contact Kevin C. Smith
City Canning
Company Spur Cross Ranch
Contact Arnold Ginsberg
City Golconda
Company
Contact Walter (Wally) Cotton
City Collingwood

New Hampshire

Company Downeast Whitewater, Inc.
Contact Rick Hoddinott
City Center Conway
Company Nereledge Inn
Contact Valerie & Dave Halpin
City North Conway
Company SKAT Outdoor Recreation
Contact George F. Haigh
City New Ipswich
Company
Contact Garry S. & Joan L. Polishan
City West Swanzey

New Jersey

Company Cedar Creek Campground
Contact Debra Fleming
City Bayville
Company Clinton Canoe & Kayak Co.
Contact Pete Pender
City Clinton
Company Jersey Paddler
Contact Walt Durrua
City Brick
Company The One That Got Away
Contact Cliff Tinsman
City Old Bridge
Company

New Mexico

Company AAA Outfitters
Contact Andrew & Annie Gonzales
City Angel Fire
Company All American Adventures
Contact Dee Charles
City Silver City
Company Back Country Hunts
Contact Steve Jones
City Carlsbad
Company Beaverhead Outfitters
Contact Jack Diamond
City Winston
Company Derringer Outfitters
Contact David & Susan Derringer
City Quemado
Company Far Flung Adventures
Contact Steve Harris
City El Prado
Company Govina Canyon Outfitters
Contact Coy Craig
City Reserve
Company Known World Guide Service
Contact John Weinmeister
City Santa Fe
Company Kokopelli Rafting Adventures
Contact Jon Asher
City Santa Fe
Company Lone Pine Hunting & Outfitters
Contact Jack Wyatt
City Chama
Company Mimbres Taxidermy & Guide Service
Contact William H. Lee
City Mimbres
Company New Wave Rafting Co.
Contact Steve Miller
City Santa Fe
Company Reserve Outfitters & Guides
Contact Bill Jernigan
City Los Lunas
Company Santa Fe Rafting ,Inc.
Contact Russell Dobson
City Santa Fe
Company Sebring's Hi Lonesome Outfitters
Contact Kerry & Deborah Sebring
City Quemado
Company Slim Randles Guide Service
Contact Slim Randles
City San Ysidro
Company Step Back Inn
Contact Karen Rapp & Tweetie Blancett
City Aztec
Company The Kauffman Group
Contact Dennis R. Kauffman
City Ruidoso
Company Vernon Tile
Contact

New York

Company Adirondack Canoe & Trail Base
Contact Alan R. "Spike" Woodruff
City Woodgate
Company Adventure Outback
Contact Tom Minchin
City Brooklyn
Company Avalanche Outdoor
Contact Kathleen J. Zyga
City Rome
Company Birchbark Tours
Contact Charles Brumley
City Saranac Lake
Company Blair's Hike & Camp
Contact Donna L. Blair
City Pottersville
Company Blue Cliffs Guiding
Contact Leslie Surprenant
City Palenville
Company Champaign Canoeing, Ltd.
Contact
City Ossining
Company Eagle Guide Service
Contact Dennis Dempsey
City Maryland
Company Earth River Expeditions
Contact Eric Hertz
City Accord
Company East Mountain Shooting Preserve
Contact Victor Vavanzo
City Dover Plains
Company Five Ponds Guide Service
Contact John Blaser
City Brewster
Company Fly Fishing with Bert & Karen
Contact Bert Darrow & Karen Graham
City Rosendale
Company Gone Fishing Guide Service
Contact Tony Ritter
City Narrowsburg
Company Laughing Bear Expeditions
Contact Steve Campbell
City Greene
Company Lockhart Guide Service
Contact Ed Lockhart
City Warrensburg
Company Lost Trail Adventures
Contact Deborah A. Grogan
City Scotia
Company Lumber City Rock Gym, Inc.
Contact John R. Baronich, Jr.
City Springville
Company Middle Earth Expeditions
Contact Wayne Failing
City Lake Placid
Company North Country Comm. College
Contact Jack Drury
City Saranac Lake
Company Northfinder
Contact Mary Kunzler-Larmann

City Canastota
Company Offshore Adventures Sea Kayaking
Contact Dave Brennan
City Williamsville
Company On Track Guide Service
Contact Peter J. Torregrossa
City Shandaken
Company Pathfinder Treks
Contact Richard E. "Rusty" Rice, Jr.
City Baldwinsville
Company Reel Easy Sportfishing
Contact Capt. Paul A. Orzolek
City Scotia
Company Rowing Thunder
Contact Karen Smith
City Paul Smiths
Company Stingray Charters
Contact Capt. Ken DeVey
City Shortsville
Company Stoney Creek Ponds Guide Service
Contact Glen A. Vandewinckel
City Webster
Company Syd & Dusty's Outfitters
Contact John Duncan
City Lake George
Company Trailhead Adventure Treks
Contact John Washburn
City Northville
Company True North Guiding
Contact Kenneth Eckhardt
City Keeseville
Company Turtle Tours & Outdoor Programs
Contact Snapper Petta
City Milford
Company
Contact Mark Dollard
City Westernville
Company
Contact Dan Drueger
City Granville
Company
Contact Richard Fabend
City LaFargeville
Company
Contact Mary Lou Graves
City Fort Ann
Company
Contact Andy Keefe
City Saratoga Springs
Company
Contact Dr. Anne LaBastille
City Westport
Company
Contact Norm Landis
City Rome
Company
Contact Kim Massari
City Saranac Lake
Company
Contact Dr. Will McPeak
City Syracuse
Company
Contact Jean-Pierre Moreau
City Syracuse
Company

Contact Michele Sellingham
City Queensbury
Company
Contact Don Tolhurst
City Liverpool

North Carolina

Company Appalachian Adventures, Inc.
Contact Jack Barrett
City Todd
Company Blue Ridge Outing Company
Contact Bob Mattingly
City Canton
Company Cape Fear Outfitters, Inc.
Contact Brad Black
City Wilmington
Company Carolina Outfitters Whitewater Rafting
Contact Billy Dills
City West Bryson City
Company Carolina Wilderness
Contact Glenn Goodrich
City Hot Spring
Company Chestnut Hunting Lodge
Contact Jerry E. Rushing
City Taylorsville
Company Davis Farms Quail Preserve
Contact Warren Davis
City Beaufort
Company Edge of the World Outfitters
Contact Greg Barrow
City Banner Elk
Company Foscoe Fishing Co. & Outfitters, Inc.
Contact Matt Fussell
City Banner Elk
Company Griffin Hill Hunting Preserve
Contact
City Wadesboro
Company High Mountain Expeditions
Contact Joyce Skaradzinski
City Blowing Rock
Company Nantahala Outdoor Center
Contact Tracy Schneider-Marketing
City Bryson City
Company Richard's Guide Service
Contact Richard Smith
City Stokesdale
Company River Runners' Retreat, Inc.
Contact Sam Hogsed
City Topton
Company Shane's Sporting Clay
Contact Shane Naylor
City Summerfield
Company Six Runs Plantation
Contact Becky Edwards
City Rose Hill
Company The National Catfishing Association (NCA)
Contact Kenne Smith
City Chapel Hill
Company Wahoos Adventures TN, Inc.
Contact Melissa France

City Boone

North Dakota

Company Centennial Charter
Contact George Zenk
City Webster
Company Club Nordak
Contact Jason Brown
City Streeter
Company Dakota Adventures Outfitters
Contact Terry Strand
City Bismarck
Company Dakota Fins, Feathers & Tails Guide Service
Contact Jim Nagel
City Bismarck
Company Hillview Hunting Acres, Inc.
Contact Bob Saunders
City Minot
Company Indian Hills Resort
Contact Byron & Tolly Holtan
City Garrison
Company Lawrence Bay Lodge
Contact Verdean and Randy Engen
City Tolna
Company Senior Goslings Goose Lodge
Contact Pete Ressler
City Bismarck
Company Terry's Guide Service
Contact Terry Focke
City Bismarck
Company The Cannonball Company
Contact Les Gion
City Regent

Ohio

Company B & B Charters
Contact Capt. Robert Duktig
City Columbia Station
Company Barney's Northcoast Charters
Contact Capt. John Barnowski
City North Royalton
Company Beluga Lou's
Contact Grace & Louis Sudano
City Berlin Center
Company Birch Bark Canoe Livery
Contact
City Urbana
Company Blue Lagoon Canoe Livery
Contact
City Butler
Company Head Hunter
Contact Capt. Jerome Abele
City Lakeside
Company Hocking Valley Canoe Livery
Contact
City Logan

Company Lake Fork Canoe & Kayak Livery
Contact
City Loudonville
Company Loudonville Canoe Livery
Contact Dick Schafrath
City Loudonville
Company Mohican Canoe Livery
Contact Chris Snively
City Loudonville
Company Mohican Reservation Canoeing
Contact
City Loudonville
Company Pleasant Valley Campground
Contact
City Loudonville
Company RiversEdge Canoe Livery & Outfitters
Contact Rhett & Andrea Rohrer
City Waynesville
Company Tallmadge Pheasant Farm & Hunting Preserve
Contact Nancy Tallmadge
City Jeromesville
Company Winke Guide Service
Contact Capt. Patrick Winke
City Port Clinton
Company Wrestle Creek Game Club
Contact Richard Hardin
City Waynesfield
Company
Contact Capt. Doris Kubinski
City Port Clinton

Oregon

Company Aces of Angling
Contact Chris Tarrant
City Eagle Point
Company Adventure Kayak
Contact Robert W. Carr, Jr.
City Bandon
Company Angling Eagle River Trips
Contact Bill F. Smith, Jr.
City Medford
Company B & B Guide Service
Contact Hal J. Borg
City Medford
Company Backcountry Outfitters
Contact Jim & Mozelle Workman
City Joseph
Company Big K Guest Ranch & Guide Service
Contact Charles Kesterson
City Elkton
Company Bill Urie Guide Service
Contact Bill Urie
City Medford
Company Black Bird Center, Inc.
Contact Mike McMullen
City Medford
Company Bob Baccus Guide Service
Contact Bob Baccus
City Medford

Company Bob's Economy Guide Service
Contact Robert L. Brown
City Hillsboro
Company Caddis Angling Shop
Contact Chris Daughters
City Eugene
Company Cascade River Runners
Contact Ron Pribble
City Klamath Falls
Company Chinook Whitewater Adventures, Inc.
Contact Tim Thornton
City Bend
Company Chrysalis Outdoors
Contact Butch Ryssdal
City Gold Beach
Company CJ Lodge
Contact Carrol L. White & Judy White
City Maupin
Company Cooley River Expeditions, Inc.
Contact Robert F. Cooley
City Albany
Company Craig Sutton's Cast & Blast
Contact Craig Sutton
City Medford
Company Crest Outward Bound School
Contact Michael J. Seeley
City Portland
Company Custom Adventure Trips
Contact Jeffrey S. Bamburg
City Portland
Company Dave Helfrich River Outfitter, Inc.
Contact Dave Helfrich
City Vida
Company Deschutes Navigation Co.
Contact Gary N. Marshall
City Madras
Company Deschutes U-Boat
Contact Tom & Donna Troutman
City Maupin
Company Deschutes Whitewater Service
Contact Robert E. Iverson
City Maupin
Company DMJ Consulting Guide
Contact Douglas M. Jones
City Scappoose
Company Don Grieve Guide Service
Contact Don Grieve
City Shady Cove
Company Doug's Guide Service
Contact Douglas A. Talmadge
City McMinnville
Company Educational Adventures Unlimited
Contact Laurence A. Lockett
City Stayton
Company Elkqua Lodge
Contact Mike & Cecilia Morris
City Elkton
Company Erekson's Outfitters
Contact Scott Erekson
City Salem
Company Ewing's Whitewater
Contact Pete Hattenhauer
City Maupin
Company Fast Water West

Contact Ron L. Altig
City Ashland
Company Fast Water West
Contact Jeff S. Little
City Ashland
Company Fast Water West
Contact Brad W. Lancaster
City Ashland
Company Fish Finder Guide Service
Contact David E. Saunders
City Grants Pass
Company Fish-Rite Boats
Contact Jamie Dorsey
City Central Point
Company Fishawk River Co.
Contact Harvey & Suzy Young
City Brookings
Company Free Spirit Rivers
Contact Dawn Jones
City Corvallis
Company Galice Resort
Contact Perry D. Robbins
City Merlin
Company Gary Kline Outfitter Guide
Contact Gary Kline
City Brookings
Company Genesis Outdoors
Contact Ken Streater
City Eugene
Company Hannah Fish Camps
Contact Denny Hannah
City Elkton
Company Harley's Guide Service
Contact Harley L. Freshour
City Brookings
Company Helfrich River Outfitters
Contact Ken R. Helfrich
City Springfield
Company Hellgate Jetboat Excursions
Contact Robert R. Hamlyn
City Grants Pass
Company Hells Canyon Adventures II, Inc.
Contact Bret & Doris Armacost
City Oxbow
Company High Country Outfitters
Contact Woody McDowell
City Joseph
Company High Desert Drifters Guides & Outfitters
Contact Rick & Kim S. Killingsworth
City Bend
Company High Desert River Outfitters
Contact Gary E. Schoenecker
City Portland
Company Hook-Up Guide Service
Contact Jack Glass
City Troutdale
Company Illahe Lodge
Contact Ernest R. Rutledge
City Agness
Company Inward Peak Kayak Instruction
Contact Kenneth M. Bavoso
City Portland
Company J. R. Amick's Guide Service
Contact James R. Amick
City Tillamook
Company Jerry's Rogue Jets

Contact Bill McNair
City Gold Beach
Company Jet Boat River Excursions
Contact William R. Cort
City Rogue River
Company Jim Dunlevy Guide Service
Contact James C. Dunlevy
City Medford
Company Jim Pringle's Guide Service
Contact James B. Pringle
City Medford
Company Jim's Guide Service
Contact James E. Whetzel
City Days Creek
Company Jim's Oregon Whitewater, Inc.
Contact Jim Berl
City McKenzie Bridge
Company Ken Martin Professional River Guide
Contact Ken Martin
City Days Creek
Company Ken Wilson Guide Service
Contact Ken Wilson
City Medford
Company King Fisher River Trips
Contact Bruce J. King
City Aloha
Company KW Guide Service
Contact Keith W. Blodgett
City Grants Pass
Company Lone Wolf Expeditions
Contact Mitchell D. McDougal
City Beaverton
Company Lower Rogue Canyon Outfitters
Contact Randall G. Nelson
City Central Point
Company Miranda's Guide Service
Contact Ed Miranda, Jr.
City Klamath Falls
Company Morang's Guide Service
Contact Michael S. Morang
City Eagle Point
Company Natural High Rafting
Contact James C. Mabry
City Beaverton
Company North West River Outfitters
Contact Craig Hughson
City Albany
Company Orange Torpedo Trips, Inc.
Contact Becky & Eric Smith
City Grants Pass
Company Orange Torpedo Trips, Inc.
Contact Donald W. Stevens
City Grants Pass
Company Oregon Ridge & River Excursions
Contact William B. Blodgett
City Glide
Company Oregon River Experiences
Contact Craig Wright
City Lake Oswego
Company Oregon Whitewater Adventures
Contact Kay & Dave Loos
City Springfield
Company Outdoor Ventures River Training & Registry

Contact Robert Grubb and William Blair
City Eugene
Company Ouzel Outfitters
Contact Kent & Beth Wickham
City Bend
Company Pacific Crest Outward Bound
Contact
City Portland
Company Paradise Bar Lodge
Contact Court Boice
City Gold Beach
Company Pat's Hand Tied Flies
Contact
City Trail
Company Peer's Snake River Rafting
Contact Darryl & Kathy Peer
City Halfway
Company Pit River Guide Service
Contact Robert H. Akins
City Shady Cove
Company Quick Silver Guide Service
Contact Richard J. Andrest
City Shady Cove
Company Rapid River Rafters
Contact Martin Smith
City Bend
Company Reachout Expeditions, Inc.
Contact Curtis A. Dunlop
City Portland
Company Reel Adventures
Contact Donald L. Schneider
City Sandy
Company Rick's Guide Service
Contact Rick Smith
City Grants Pass
Company Rippling Brook Flyfishing Outfitters
Contact Rich Youngers
City Salem
Company River Riders, Inc.
Contact
City Hood River
Company River Visions Adventure Company
Contact John G. Trujillo
City Salem
Company Rogue River Guide Service
Contact Paul Lopes
City Grants Pass
Company Rogue River Mail Boat Trips
Contact Ed & Sue Kammer
City Gold Beach
Company Rogue River Raft Trips
Contact Michelle Hanten
City Merlin
Company Rogue River Safaris
Contact Garrett F. Combs
City Wedderburn
Company Rogue Wilderness, Inc.
Contact Robert R. Rafalovich
City Grants Pass
Company Rogue/Klamath River Adventures
Contact Warren D. & Terri Helgeson
City Eagle Point
Company Ron Dungey & Sons
Contact Ronald F. Dungey
City Grants Pass

Company Ron Jones Guide Service
Contact Ron Jones
City Medford
Company Roundy's River Trips
Contact Dave Roundy
City Eagle Point
Company Siskiyou Adventures, Inc.
Contact Eric Peterson
City Jacksonville
Company Solitude River Trips
Contact Al & Jeana Bukowsky
City Merlin
Company Southern Oregon River Trips
Contact Brian J. Wager
City Medford
Company Specialty Tackle & Guide Service
Contact Curt Thompson
City Central Point
Company Steve Beyerlin Guide Service
Contact Robert S. Beyerlin
City Gold Beach
Company Sun Country Tours, Inc.
Contact Dennis Oliphant
City Bend
Company The Big K Guest Ranch
Contact Kathie Williamson
City Elkton
Company The Oregon Angler
Contact Todd Hannah
City Elkton
Company The Oregon Paddler
Contact Michael G. Hussey
City Springfield
Company Tightliness
Contact Jeff and Laura Helfrich
City Vida
Company Tom Richardson's Rogue Guide Service
Contact Thomas P. Richardson
City Medford
Company Village Baptist Church
Contact Scott A. Mauck
City Hillsboro
Company Water Pony River Tours
Contact Nancy A. Fiegel
City Lostine
Company White Horse Rafting
Contact Bruce P. Brunoe, Jr.
City Warm Springs
Company Wild River Adventures
Contact Carollyn Staley
City Gold Beach
Company Willie Boats, Inc.
Contact Willie Illingworth
City Central Point
Company Wy'East Expeditions
Contact Michael R. Gehrman
City Mt. Hood
Company
Contact James J. Armstrong
City Portland
Company
Contact Edward (Skip) Baldwin, Jr.
City Harbor
Company
Contact Bob Bauer
City Wilsonville

Company
Contact Robert W. Boehm
City Eagle Point
Company
Contact Vince Bogard
City Medford
Company
Contact Paul Brown
City Medford
Company
Contact Jim Buck
City Medford
Company
Contact Jim Calhoun
City Medford
Company
Contact Pat Cameron
City Grants Pass
Company
Contact Ted Camp
City Grants Pass
Company
Contact Win Charlton
City Medford
Company
Contact Kent Clark
City Medford
Company
Contact Bill Colley
City Central Point
Company
Contact Don Davidson
City Klamath Falls
Company
Contact Roy Doe
City Medford
Company
Contact James P. Donovan
City Ashland
Company
Contact Hayden A. Glatte, III
City Ashland
Company
Contact Marc Grieve
City Prospect
Company
Contact David Grieve
City Trail
Company
Contact Gene Gros
City Eagle Point
Company
Contact Dave Hendry
City Medford
Company
Contact Don Hinton
City Rogue River
Company
Contact Greg Ingram
City Medford
Company
Contact Ed Inman
City Central Point
Company
Contact Richard Jorgensen
City Talent
Company
Contact John E. Judy

City Camp Sherman
Company
Contact Marilyn Kalstad
City Eugene
Company
Contact Larry L. Kent
City Prospect
Company
Contact James D. Klusman
City Agness
Company
Contact Boyd Kramer
City Eagle Point
Company
Contact Bob Kramer
City Medford
Company
Contact Terry L. McCord
City Grants Pass
Company
Contact Don Nelson
City Riddle
Company
Contact Michael D. O'Connors
City Medford
Company
Contact John E. Odegard
City Gresham
Company
Contact Rick Piscitello
City Brookings
Company
Contact Patrick E. Reichner
City Gladstone
Company
Contact Gary Rhinehart
City Medford
Company
Contact Kenny C. Richardson
City Gresham
Company
Contact Michael Siewell
City Central Point
Company
Contact Eugene Smith
City Medford
Company
Contact James M. Staight
City Springfield
Company
Contact Jason Tarrant
City Corvallis
Company
Contact Steve Tichenor
City Grants Pass
Company
Contact Jim Valentine
City Rogue River
Company
Contact Jimmy R. Varner
City Shady Cove
Company
Contact Chris Young
City Prospect

Pennsylvania

Company Adventure Sports Canoe &
Raft Trips
Contact
City Marshalls Creek
Company Bucks County River Country
Contact
City Point Pleasant
Company Chamberlain Canoes, Rafts,
Tubes
Contact
City Minisink Hills
Company Fishing Creek Outfitters
Contact Dave Colley
City Benton
Company Greater Pittsburg Gun Club
Contact Tex
City Bulger
Company Jim Thorpe River Adventures,
Inc.
Contact Bob Kuhn
City Jim Thorpe
Company Kittatinny Canoes
Contact Dave Jones & Ruth Jones
City Dingmans Ferry
Company Laurel Highlands River Tours,
Inc.
Contact Mark McCarty & Terry Palmo
City Ohiopyle
Company Mountain Streams & Trails
Outfitters
Contact
City Ohiopyle
Company Pine Creek Outfitters, Inc.
Contact Chuck Dillon
City Wellsboro
Company Pocono Whitewater, Ltd.
Contact Doug Fogal
City Jim Thorpe
Company Smith Game Farm
Contact
City Sarver
Company The Preserve
Contact
City Milford
Company Valley Forge Canoe, Tube &
Rafting
Contact
City Monocacy
Company White Water Adventurers, Inc.
Contact Robert Marietta, Sr.
City Ohiopyle
Company Whitewater Challengers, Inc.
Contact Ken Powley
City White Haven
Company Whitewater Rafting
Adventures, Inc.
Contact Joe Flyzik & Stephen Behun
City Albrightsville
Company Whitewater Rafting, Inc.
Contact
City White Haven
Company Wild and Scenic River Tours
Contact
City Lackawaxen
Company Wilderness Voyageurs, Inc.

Contact Chris Burke
City Ohiopyle
Company Windy Ridge Game Farm &
Kennel
Contact Robert Stewart
City Tioga
Company Youghiogheny Outfitters, Inc.
Contact Stuart VanNosdein
City Ohiopyle

Rhode Island

Company Four-Point Canoe Outfitters
Contact Gary Point
City Barrington

South Carolina

Company Back 40 Wing & Clay, Inc.
Contact Grady Roscoe
City Bethune
Company Back Woods Quail Club
Contact Edsel Hemingway
City Georgetown
Company Cattooga River Adventures
Contact
City Long Creek
Company Chattooga River Adventures,
Inc.
Contact Ann Boomhower
City Mountain Rest
Company Hoyett's Grocery & Tackle
Contact Dessie and Paul Orr
City Salem
Company Jackie Jones Guide Service
Contact Jackie Jones
City Cross
Company Lake Marion Guide Service
Contact Donnie Baker, Sr.
City Sumter
Company M & M Kayak Adventures
Contact Adam Masters & Tristan
Mahaffey
City Easley
Company Mountain Lakes Vacation
Center
Contact Joan & John Carter
City Fair Play
Company River Bend Sportsman's
Resort
Contact Ralph Brendle
City Fingerville
Company Ship's Guide Service
Contact Captain Steve Shipley
City Santee
Company Wildwater Ltd. Rafting
Contact Jack Wise/Jeff Greiner
City Long Creek
Company

Contact Frank Drose
City Manninig
Company
Contact John Sellers
City Cross

South Dakota

Company ALP Hunting
Contact Adolph & LaVonne Peterson
City Elkton
Company B & B Guide Service
Contact Bruce D. Baker & Craig Novak
City Pierre
Company Diamond Dot Ranch
Contact Linda Denbeste
City Reliance
Company Etzkorn's Goose Camp
Contact Terry Etzkorn & Darrel Canode
City Pierre
Company Great Plains Hunting
Contact Clyde L. Zepp
City Wessington
Company High Plains Game Ranch
Contact Randy & Rhonda Vallery
City Nisland
Company Paul Nelson Farm
Contact Paul Nelson
City Gettysburg
Company Shattuck Hunting Service
Contact Darrell Shattuck
City Gregory
Company Spring Creek Guides
Contact Adam Knoepfle
City Artas
Company Spring Creek Resort
Contact John Brakss & Rick Ray
City Pierre
Company Triple H Hunting Service
Contact Marlin & Marilyn Haukaas
City Colome

Tennessee

Company Adventures Unlimited
Contact Carlo & Julie Smith
City Ocoee
Company Alpha Adventures YMCA
Contact Karen Galloway
City Maryville
Company Bo's Landing
Contact Bo Bentley
City Tiptonville
Company Cedar Hill Resort
Contact Ron Roberts
City Celina
Company Cherokee Adventures, Inc.
Contact Dennis Nedelman
City Erwin

Company Cherokee Rafting, Inc.
Contact John & Judy Thomason
City Ocoee
Company Cripple Creek Expeditions
Contact Roger Scott
City Ocoee
Company High Country Adventures
Contact Rayland Lilley
City Ocoee
Company Hiwassee Scenic River
Outfitters, Inc.
Contact David Smith
City Reliance
Company Ocoee Inn Rafting, Inc.
Contact Jerry Hamby
City Benton
Company Ocoee Outdoors
Contact J.T. Lemons
City Ocoee
Company Outdoor Adventure Rafting
O.A.R.
Contact Doug Simmons
City Ocoee
Company Pigeon River Outdoors
Contact Claudette Geoffrion
City Gatlinburg
Company Quest Expeditions
Contact Keith Jenkins
City Benton
Company Rafting, Inc.
Contact Roger Scott
City Ocoee
Company Rapid Descent River Company
Contact Jerry Kader
City Hartford
Company Russell Fork Expeditions
Contact Channing Dale & Laureatte Loy
City Shady Valley
Company Smokey Mountain
Expeditions, Inc.
Contact Roger Scott
City Ocoee
Company Smoky Mountain Outdoors,
Unltd.
Contact Jeff Reed
City Hartford
Company Sunburst Adventures, Inc.
Contact Larry Guy
City Benton
Company The Ocoee Adventure
Company
Contact Larry Mashburn
City Cleveland
Company The Whitewater Company
Contact Scott Strausbaugh
City Hartford
Company Webb Brothers Float Service,
Inc.
Contact Harold Webb
City Reliance

Texas

Company Angelina Grocery

Contact Dan Williamson
City Jasper
Company Armstrong Outfitters
Contact Kirk R. Armstrong
City Denton
Company Awesom Adventures
Contact Ray "Bear" Rutzen
City Austwell
Company Big Bend River Tours
Contact Beth Garcia
City Terlingua
Company Bland's Fishing Guide Service
Contact Wayne Bland
City Livingston
Company Circle H Ranch
Contact Charlie Harris
City George West
Company Fat Daddy's Outdoors
Unlimited
Contact William E. Horn
City Alba
Company Foster Ranch Kennels &
Outfitters
Contact Jim & Debbie Foster
City Los Fresnos
Company Johnston Guide Statement
Contact Stephen W. Johnston
City Hemphill
Company Lake Fork Lodge
Contact Kyle Jones
City Alba
Company Rio Paisano Ranch
Contact Casey Taub
City Riviera
Company Saltwater Addiction
Contact Captain Joe M. Mosley
City Bay City
Company South Bay Guide Service
Contact Gordon S. Spears, III
City Aransas Pass
Company Texas River Expeditions
Contact Greg Henington
City Terlingua
Company TNT
Contact Jack P. Justus, Jr.
City Friendswood
Company Tom's Guide Service
Contact Thomas W. Ranft
City Graford
Company WaterFowl Specialties, Inc.
Contact Terry Karstedt
City El Campo
Company
Contact Scott A. Boone
City Quitman
Company
Contact Billy Carter
City Uncertain
Company
Contact Frederick Hoyt
City Rockport
Company
Contact Clark A. Miles
City Port Aransas
Company
Contact Marc R. Mitchell
City Sulphur Spring
Company

Contact Michael J. Moody
City Alba
Company
Contact Captain Dewitt Thomas
City Port Isabel
Company
Contact Gary Dean Tinnerman
City Aransas Pass
Company
Contact Carl (Edward) Wentrcek
City Corpus Christi
Company
Contact Ken Williams
City Graford
Company
Contact James A. Williams
City Quitman

Utah

Company Adrift Adventures/Myke
Hughes
Contact Myke Hughes
City Moab
Company Adventure River Expeditions
Contact Skip Bell
City Moab
Company Big Rock Candy Mountain
River Trips
Contact
City Marysvale
Company Canyon Voyages
Contact Don Oblak
City Moab
Company Canyonlands by Night
Contact
City Moab
Company Canyonlands Field Institute
Contact Karla VanderZanden
City Moab
Company Colorado River & Trail
Expeditions
Contact David Mackay
City Salt Lake City
Company Deer Springs Ranch
Contact Larry Clarkson
City Kanab
Company Dinosaur River Expeditions
Contact Tim Mertens
City Park City
Company Don & Meg Hatch River
Expeditions
Contact Meg Hatch
City Vernal
Company Eagle Outdoor Sports
Contact
City Kaysville
Company Eagle Outdoor Sports
Contact Doug Smith
City Bountiful
Company Falcon's Ledge Lodge/
Altamont Flyfishers
Contact
City Altamont

Company Grand Canyon Bar 10 Ranch
Contact
City St. George
Company Grand Canyon Expeditions Co.
Contact Michael Denoyer
City Kanab
Company Hatch River Expeditions, Inc.
Contact Clark Hatch
City Vernal
Company Hatt's Ranch
Contact Royd Hatt
City Green River
Company High Desert Adventures, Inc.
Contact Mark Sleight
City St. George
Company Holiday River Expeditions
Contact Dee Holladay
City Salt Lake City
Company La Sal Mountain Guest Ranch
Contact Sunny & Hardy Redd
City LaSal
Company Lake Powell Tours, Inc.
Contact
City St. George
Company Mark Sleight Expeditions, Inc.
Contact
City St. George
Company Moab Rafting Co.
Contact
City Moab
Company Moki Mac River Expeditions
Contact Anna Lee Quist
City Salt Lake City
Company Navtec Expeditions
Contact John Williams & Chris Williams
City Moab
Company Nichols Expeditions, Inc.
Contact Judy Nichols
City Moab
Company North American River &
Canyonlands Tours
Contact
City Moab
Company Peak River Expeditions
Contact
City West Jordan
Company Red River Canoe Co.
Contact Bruce Keeler
City Moab
Company Red Rock River Co., Inc.
Contact Rob A. Bero
City Salt Lake City
Company Redd Ranches Guides &
Outfitters
Contact David Redd
City La Sal
Company Sheri Griffith Expeditions, Inc.
Contact Sheri Griffith
City Moab
Company Tag-A-Long Expeditions
Contact Bob Jones
City Moab
Company Ted Hatch River Expeditions,
Inc.
Contact Ted Hatch
City Vernal
Company Three Green Outfitters
Contact James Ryan Stone

City Smithfield
Company Tour West, Whitewater Adventure
Contact
City Orem
Company Western River Expeditions
Contact
City Moab
Company Western River Expeditions, Inc.
Contact Brian Merrill
City Moab
Company Wild Adventures
Contact
City Moab
Company Willow Creek Kennels & Guide Service
Contact Kelly Laier
City Salina
Company World Wide River Expeditions
Contact Richard Jones
City Midvale

Vermont

Company Adventure Guides of Vermont
Contact Graydon Stevens
City North Ferrisburgh
Company Battenkill Canoe, Ltd.
Contact
City Arlington
Company National Audubon Society
Contact Stephen Young
City Waitsfield
Company Outdoor Adventure of Vermont
Contact Hal Leyshon
City Montpelier
Company Uncle Jammer's Guide Service
Contact James Ehlers
City Underhill
Company Vermont Worldwide Adventures
Contact Dana Leavitt
City Lyndon

Virginia

Company Front Royal Canoe
Contact Don Roberts
City Front Royal
Company Richmond Raft Company
Contact Stuart Bateman
City Richmond
Company Trout & About
Contact Phil Gay
City Arlington
Company Wilderness Odysseys, Ltd.

Contact David Koritko
City Alexandria

Washington

Company AAA Rafting
Contact Jon A. Hall
City Husum
Company All Rivers Adventures
Contact Bruce Carlson
City Cashmere
Company Alpine Adventures
Contact
City Leavenworth
Company Blue Mountain Adventure Company & Lodge
Contact David Fiala
City Beldlevue
Company Cascade Adventures, Inc.
Contact Rocco Altobelli
City Seattle
Company Cascade Corrals
Contact Cragg Courtney
City Stehekin
Company Cascade Fishing Adventure, Inc.
Contact Dana C. Bottcher
City Seattle
Company Cooke Canyon Hunt Club
Contact Ed Nestler-President
City Ellensburg
Company Downstream River Runners
Contact Casey & Karen Garland
City Monroe
Company Icicle Outfitters & Guides
Contact Bruce & Sandy Wick
City Leavenworth
Company Island Institute
Contact
City Friday Harbor
Company Kain's Fishing Adventures, Inc.
Contact Captain Greg Kain
City Puyallup
Company Landt Farms Shooting Preserve
Contact Elwood Landt
City Nine Mile Falls
Company NCAT Whitewater
Contact John & Debbie Rivard
City Kennewick
Company Osprey Rafting Co.
Contact Gary Planagan
City Leavenworth
Company Reachout Expeditions
Contact Paul Spence
City Anacortes
Company Redline River Adventures
Contact Jerry Reddell
City Darington
Company Renegade River Rafters
Contact Mark H. Hughey
City Stevenson
Company River Riders
Contact Jim Behla

City Pateros
Company Riverspirit Spa
Contact Elizabeth P. Case
City Mount Vernon
Company Sawtooth Outfitters
Contact Brian Varrelman
City Pateros
Company WaveTrek
Contact Chris Jonason
City Index
Company Wild & Scenic River Tours
Contact Allan S. Kearney
City Seattle
Company Wildwater River Tours
Contact Rodney H. Amundson
City Federal Way

West Virginia

Company Ace Whitewater, Ltd.
Contact Jerry Cook & Ernest Kincaid
City Oak Hill
Company Adventure Expeditions/New River Rafting
Contact Jack Tolliver
City Glen Jean
Company Alpine Bible Camp
Contact Kim Buttram
City Bradley
Company Appalachian Wildwaters, Inc.
Contact Imre Szilagyi
City Rowlesburg
Company Blackwater Outdoor Center
Contact George Bright & Jim Browning
City St. George
Company Blue Ridge Outfitters, Inc.
Contact Peter Bruan
City Harpers Ferry
Company Cacapon Canoe Company
Contact Woodrow E. Taylor
City Great Cacapon
Company Cheat River Outfitters, Inc.
Contact Erik A. Neilson
City Albright
Company Class VI River Runners, Inc.
Contact David Arnold & Jeff Proctor
City Lansing
Company Class VI, Ltd.
Contact Doug Proctor
City Lansing
Company Coal River Canoe Livery, LTD
Contact John & Dorris E. Walls
City Alum Creek
Company Drift-A-Bit, Inc.
Contact Kirk McKown-General Mgr.
City Fayetteville
Company Eagle's Nest Outfitters
Contact Arvella Zimmerer
City Petersburg
Company Historical River Tours
Contact Eric Neilson
City Harpers Ferry
Company Milleson's Walnut Grove Campground

Contact Nannette E. Milleson
City Springfield
Company Mountain Connections
Contact Chris Ellis
City Charleston
Company Mountain River Tours, Inc.
Contact Michael Gray
City Hico
Company Mountain State Outdoor
Center, Inc.
Contact David Arnold & Jeff Proctor
City Lansing
Company New & Gauley River
Adventures, Inc.
Contact Lora Adkins and Owner: Skip
Heater
City Lansing
Company North American River Rafters,
Inc.
Contact Frank M. Lukacs
City Hico
Company Passage to Adventure, Inc.
Contact Benji Simpson
City Fayetteville
Company River Riders, Inc.
Contact Mark W. Grimes
City Harpers Ferry
Company Rivers
Contact Eddie Lilly
City Lansing
Company Rivers II
Contact Karen Calvert & Eddie Lilly
City Lansing
Company Sandstone Jet Boats, Inc.
Contact Jon Dragan
City Thurmond
Company Scott's Cabins & Canoe Rentals
Contact Steven A. Schetrom
City Fisher
Company Songer Whitewater, Inc.
Contact Len Hanger
City Fayetteville
Company The Rivermen, Inc.
Contact Owen Campbell
City Lansing
Company Trough General Store
Contact Rosscoe B. Dean
City Romney
Company USA Raft, Inc.
Contact Imre Szilagyi & David Robinson
City Rowlesburg
Company West Virginia Whitewater, Inc.
Contact Randy Jenkins & Dearl Johnson
City Fayetteville
Company Wildwater Expeditions
Unlimited
Contact K. Chris Dragan
City Lansing
Company
Contact Dr. Van F. Anderson
City Morgantown

Wisconsin

Company A-Ahoy Lucky Boy Fishing
Charters
Contact Capts. Eddie & Shirley Szukalski
City Milwaukee
Company Dog Skin Lake Lodge &
Outpost
Contact John Slater
City Turtle Lake
Company Hawe Hunting Preserve
Contact
City Waldo
Company Hawk's Nest Turtle Flambeau
Outfitters
Contact Dave Pucci
City St. Germain
Company K & S Charters
Contact Capt. Karl Schmidt
City Fond du Lac
Company Kosir's Rapid Rafts
Contact Dan Kosir
City Athelstane
Company Namekagon Outfitters
Contact Mike Krieger
City Trego
Company Oakwood Kennel & Game
Farm
Contact Ron Norman
City Allenton
Company Outdoors with Mic
Contact
City Butternut
Company Palmquist's "The Farm"
Contact
City Brantwood
Company R V Charters Corp.
Contact Kevin Naze & Judy Meyers
City Algoma
Company Riverside Canoes & Kayaks
Contact Jim
City Eau Claire
Company Spoonfeeder II Charters
Contact Capt. Brian Saari
City Port Wing
Company U Charters
Contact Capt. Randy Even
City Sheboygan
Company Wild River Outfitters
Contact Jerry Dorff
City Grantsburg

Wyoming

Company Barker-Ewing River Trips
Contact Frank Ewing
City Jackson
Company Barker-Ewing Scenic Float
Trips
Contact
City Moose
Company Bridger Wilderness Outfitters
Contact Tim Singwald
City Pinedale

Company Broken Horseshoe Outfitters
Contact William Carr
City Buffalo
Company Circle S Outfitters
Contact Don Smith
City Farson
Company Coy's Yellow Creek Outfitting
Contact B. Joe Coy
City Cody
Company Crossed Sabres Ranch
Contact Fred Norris
City Wapiti
Company Dave Hansen Whitewater
Contact
City Jackson
Company Diamond D Ranch-Outfitters
Contact Rod Doty
City Moran
Company Elk Ridge Outfitters
Contact Terry Reach
City Pinedale
Company Flying A Ranch
Contact Debbie Hansen
City Pinedale
Company Green River Guest Ranch
Outfitters
Contact Phillip Reints Jr.
City Cora
Company Haderlie's Tincup Mt. Guest
Ranch
Contact David & Lorie Haderlie
City Freedom
Company High Mountain Adventures
Contact Lamont Merritt
City Afton
Company High Mountain Horseback
Adventure
Contact Fern White
City Cheyenne
Company High Mountain Outfitters
Contact Robert Deroche
City Cody
Company Horse Creek Ranch/Billings
Enterprises
Contact Ray Billings
City Jackson
Company J.T. Tinney Outfitting
Contact James T. Tinney
City Lovell
Company Jackson Hole Llamas
Contact Jill
City Jackson
Company Jackson Hole Whitewater
Contact
City Jackson
Company Lewis & Clark River
Expeditions
Contact
City Jackson
Company Little Bighorn Outfitters
Contact Tim Moyes
City Sheridan
Company Magic Mountains Outfitters
Contact S.(Sharon) R. Dayton
City Cokeville
Company Milliron 2 Outfitting
Contact Billy Sinclair
City Worland

Company Platt's Guides & Outfitters
Contact Ronald R. Platt
City Encampment
Company Raven Creek Outfitters
Contact Kent Drake
City Gillette
Company Sand Creek Outfitters
Contact Jim P. Collins
City Alcova
Company Sand Wild Water, Inc.
Contact Charles Sands
City Wilson
Company Sanke River Kayak & Canoe School
Contact
City Jackson Hole
Company Snake River Institute
Contact
City Wilson
Company Snake River Park, Inc.
Contact Stan & Karen Chatham
City Jackson
Company Solitude Float Trips, Inc.
Contact
City Moose
Company Spotted Horse Ranch
Contact Clare Berger
City Jackson Hole
Company The HOLE Hiking Experience, Inc.
Contact Cathy Shill
City Jackson
Company Triple Creek Hunts
Contact Jim Freeburn
City Fort Laramie
Company Turpin Meadow Ranch
Contact Stan Castagno
City Moran
Company UXU Ranch
Contact Hamilton Bryan
City Wapiti
Company Wolf Mountain Outfitters
Contact Guy Azevedo
City Afton
Company Wyoming Rivers & Trails
Contact Liz & Matt David
City Pinedale
Company Wyoming Wilderness Outfitters
Contact Jake Kay Clark
City Powell
Company Yellowstone Troutfitters
Contact Steve Perry
City Cody

Canada

Alberta

Company Amethyst Lakes/Tonquin Valley Pack Trips
Contact Wald & Lavone Olson
City Brule
Company Anchor D High Mountain

Hunts, Ltd.
Contact Dewy Matthews
City Black Diamond
Company Buffalo Lake Outfitters
Contact Brad Steinhoff
City Donalda
Company Classic Outfitters
Contact Jim Hole Jr.
City Edmonton
Company Del Bredeson Guiding & Outfitting
Contact Del Bredeson
City Grande Prairie
Company Diamond Jim Mountain Rides
Contact Jim Colosimo
City Rocky Mountain House
Company Don Ayers Outfitters
Contact Don & Tuffy Ayers
City Edmonton
Company Double H Outfitters
Contact Heather & Herb Bailey
City Stony Plain
Company Great Plains Outfitters
Contact Darryl Giesbrecht
City Medicine Hat
Company High Country Vacations
Contact Bazil Leonard & Susan Feddema
City Grande Cache
Company McMillan River Outfitters
Contact Dave Coleman
City Grovedale
Company Nahanni Wilderness Adventures, Ltd.
Contact David Hibbard
City Didsbury
Company North Alberta Outfitters
Contact Troy & Lisa Foster
City Slave Lake
Company North Alta Ventures
Contact Dollard & Shelly Dallaire
City North Star
Company Northern Wilderness Outfitters
Contact Weldon & Marilyn Prosser
City Slave Lake
Company Saddle Peak Trail Rides
Contact Dave Richards
City Cochrane

British Columbia

Company Arctic Waterways/Whitewolf Adventure
Contact Barry Beales
City Port Coquitlam
Company Bogie Mtn./Besa River Outfitters
Contact Paul Gillis
City Fort Nelson
Company Canadian River Expeditions
Contact
City Whistler
Company Chilcotin River Guide Outfitter
Contact William Mulvahill

City Alexis Creek
Company Coastal Inlet Adventures
Contact
City Shawnigan Lake
Company Great Canadian Ecoventures
Contact Tom Faess
City Vancouver
Company Mackenzie Mountain Outfitters
Contact Stan Stevens
City Toms Lake
Company Sidka Tours
Contact
City Atlin
Company The Blackwater Company
Contact Ron Thompson
City Williams Lake

Labrador

Company True North Outfitting Co.
Contact Jim Hudson
City Goose Bay

Manitoba

Company AJ Tours
Contact Craig Dunn
City Winnipeg
Company Barron Land Outfitters
Contact Joe Barron
City Churchill
Company Batstone Canoe Pick-Up
Contact Jack Batstone
City Churchill
Company Churchill Wilderness Encounter
Contact Bonnie Chartier
City Churchill
Company Clearwater Canoe Outfitters
Contact Doug Sangster
City The Pas
Company Crooked Creek Lodge/Delta Marsh Canoe
Contact John & Marlene Lavallee
City St. Ambroise
Company Dan's Outfitting
Contact B. Danny Gudbjartson
City Gimli
Company Dymond Lake Outfitters Ltd.
Contact Doug Webber
City Thompson
Company Experience Tours
Contact Bob Reid
City Winnipeg
Company Fraser Family Farms
Contact Ernest & Donna Fraser
City Fairfax
Company Frontiers North

Contact Merv & Lynda Gunter
City Winnipeg
Company Grass River Outfitters
Contact Rick & Wendy Hall
City Wabowden
Company Lakeside Outfitters
Contact Gerry Vermette
City Winnipegosis
Company Lazy River Paddlers
Contact Roland Gatin & Kirk Mohamed
City Winnipeg
Company Manitoba Buck Masters
Contact William Friesen
City San Clara
Company Maurice's Sportsman
Outfitters
Contact Maurice or Sandra Thibert
City Cayer
Company Mink Creek Outfitters
Contact Mike Dudar
City Ethelbert
Company Mistik Creek Canoe
Adventures
Contact Thomas G. & Mikeal P.
Nevakshonoff
City Flin Flon
Company North River Outfitters
Contact Jack & Darlene Crolly
City Thompson
Company Northern Manitoba Outfitters
Contact Jack & Georgia Clarkson
City Berens River
Company Paddling Pursuits
Contact Pat Barker & Perry McGregor
City Winnipeg
Company Raven Eye Outfitters
Contact Garth Duncan & Karin Aldinger
City Winnipeg
Company Riverview Lodge
Contact Irene & Pat Blaney
City Seven Sisters Falls
Company Sasa-Ginni-Gak Lodge
Contact Naomi Johnsons
City Arnes
Company Silence of the North
Contact Harold Kirtzinger & Marian
Schlosser
City Flin Flon
Company Souris River Adventures
Contact Bob Caldweld
City Deloraine
Company The New Vickery Lodge
Contact Rick & Fran Hubbs
City The Pas
Company Turtle Mountain Outfitting
Contact Don & Lynn Smith
City Killarney
Company Walking River Guiding &
Outfitting
Contact Bev Murphy & Gerald Walker
City Eriksdale
Company Wanipigow Wilderness
Adventures
Contact Jean Zeiner
City Winnipeg
Company Whiteshell Lake Resort
Contact Liberty & David DesRoches-
Dueck

City Whitemouth
Company Whitetail Outfitters
Contact Darlene & Justin Giasson
City Fisher Branch
Company Wild-Wise, Inc.
Contact Wild-Wise Program
City Winnipeg
Company Wilderness Adventures
Contact Les Tripp
City The Pas
Company Wilderness Instruction Plus
Contact Roger Conrad
City Brandon
Company Windsock Lodge/Hastings
Bros. Outfitters
Contact Tim & Donna Hastings
City Bissett

New Brunswick

Company Black Bear Lodge
Contact Gilbert Pelletier
City Millcove
Company Cedar Creek Hunting Camp
Contact George Kennedy
City Moores Mills
Company Fundy Outfitters
Contact Malcolm Rossiter
City Alma
Company Henderson's Hunting Camps,
Ltd.
Contact Stephanie & Clarence Walton
City Hartland
Company True North Adventures
Contact Thomas Barrett
City Back Bay
Company Upper Oxbow Adventures
Contact Debbie Norton
City Trout Brook
Company Walt's Guiding & Outfitting
Contact Walter & Betty Mallery
City King's Co.

Newfoundland

Company Clarenville Aviation Ltd.
Contact Neil Pelley
City Shoal Harbour
Company Cloud River Outfitters
Contact Alvin Colbourne
City Roddickton
Company Iron Bound Outfitters
Contact George Payne
City Parson's Pond
Company Ocean Side Country Lodge
Contact Chris Rowsell
City Point Leamington
Company Strawberry Hill Resort Ltd.
Contact Dan McCarthy

City St. John's
Company Wilderness Outfitters
Contact Gene Mercer
City St. John's

Northwest Territories

Company Arctic Nature Tours, Ltd.
Contact Fred Carmichael & Miki O'Kane
City Inuvik
Company Arctic Tour Company
Contact Winnie & Roger Gruben
City Inuvik
Company Aurora Sport Fishing & Tours
Contact
City Fort Providence
Company Banks Island Big Game Hunts
Contact Sachs Harbour HTC
City Sachs Harbour
Company Canoe Arctic, Inc.
Contact Alex Hall
City Ft. Smith
Company Ch'ii Adventures Ltd.
Contact
City Fort McPherson
Company Dempster Patrol Outfitters
Contact Keith Colin
City Fort McPherson
Company Eagle Nest Tours
Contact Arthur Beck
City Hay River
Company Enodah Wilderness Travel Ltd.
Contact Ragnar & Doreen Wesstrom
City Yellowknife
Company Jackson's Arctic Circle Tours
Contact Wilfred Jackson
City Fort Good Hope
Company North-Wright Air. Ltd.
Contact
City Norman Wells
Company Old Town Float Base
Contact Yvonne Quick
City Yellowknife
Company Ookpik Tours & Adventures
Contact James & Maureen Pokiak
City Tuktoyaktuk
Company Rendezvous Lake Outpost
Camp
Contact Billy Jacobson
City Tuktoyaktuk
Company Taiga Tour Company
Contact Clayton Burke
City Fort Smith

Ontario

Company Adventure Canada
Contact
City Mississauga

Company Algonquin Outfitters
Contact The Swift Family
City Dwight
Company Andy Lake Resort
Contact Marc & Judy Bechard
City Kenora
Company Biscotasting Sportsman Lodge
Contact Eddie Peters
City Biscotasting
Company Black Feather Wilderness Adventures
Contact Wendy Grater
City Parry Sound
Company Camp Conewango
Contact Doug Lynett
City Redbridge
Company Camp Quetico
Contact Marshall & Karen Manns
City Atikokan
Company Canoe Canada Outfitters & Outpost Cabins
Contact Bud Dickson & Jim Clark
City Atikokan
Company Canoe North Adventures
Contact Lin Ward & Al Pace
City Orangeville
Company Chippawa Lodge
Contact Donald, Amy & Andrew Dunn Janet
City Barry's Bay
Company Colimar Lodge
Contact Fran Koning
City Jellicoe Ontario
Company Cosy Cove Cottages
Contact Linda & Bud Link
City Callander
Company Elephant Lake Lodge
Contact Bill & Sandy Smith
City Harcourt
Company Ennismore Inn & Resort
Contact Garry & Judy Mattis
City Peterborough
Company Ernie's Cottages & Campground
Contact Ernie Martel
City Missanabie
Company Fish Tale Lodge
Contact Richard & Nancy Sherborn
City Noelville
Company Fleming's Black Bear Outpost Camps
Contact Walter Fleming
City Jellicoe
Company Forbe's Holiday Resort
Contact Bill & Ellen Kloepfer
City Whitefish Falls
Company Fox Lake Lodge
Contact Vickie & Dave Ormerod
City Levack
Company Hanson's Wilderness Lodges Ltd.
Contact Maureen and Randy Hansons
City Nestor Falls
Company Hay Lake Lodge
Contact Erin & Phil Morlock
City Whitney
Company Hillsport Wilderness Hunting Camps

Contact Mark & Karen Stephenson
City Longlac
Company Holiday Haven
Contact Ernie & Sharon Kormendi
City Manitowaning
Company Huron Air & Outfitters Inc.
Contact Donna & Ernie Nicholl
City Armstrong
Company Indianhead Lodge, Ltd.
Contact Tim & Karen McNanney
City Sioux Narrows
Company James Bay Frontier Travel Assoc.
Contact Guy Lamarche
City Schumacher
Company James Bay Goose Camp
Contact Charlie Wynne
City Kaskechewan
Company Lady Evelyn Outfitting Ltd.
Contact Ted & Leona Krofchak
City Temagami
Company Lakeview Resort
Contact John & Julie VanVeen
City Kagawong
Company Madawaska Kanu Centre
Contact Claudia & Dirk Van Wijk
City Barry's Bay
Company Manotak Lodge
Contact Rej Roy
City Perrault Falls
Company Moose Horn Lodge
Contact Roxann Lynn
City Chapleau
Company Munro Park
Contact May Munro
City Powassan
Company Northern Comfort Wilderness Adventures
Contact The Coscos
City Sioux Lookout
Company Northern Lights Resort
Contact The Millers
City Nolalu
Company Northern Wilderness Outfitters
Contact Bev & Bill MacFarlane
City South River
Company Northwinds Canadian Outfitters
Contact Rod & Gail Munford
City Vermilion Bay
Company O-Pee-Chee Lake Lodge
Contact Siobhan & Gord Rolland
City Marten River
Company Opeongo Mountain Resort
Contact Bob & Chris Peltzer
City Eganville
Company Panorama Camp
Contact Denis & Ginette Rainville
City Lavigne
Company Pine Acres Resort & Outfitters
Contact Rene & Joyce Lavoie
City Vermilion Bay
Company Resort Tapatoo
Contact Christa & Guenter Siebert
City Parry Sound
Company Ridgewood Cottages
Contact Tom Byers

City Temagami
Company Sandy Point Camp
Contact Bill & Penny Higgins
City Dryden
Company Smoothwater Outfitters
Contact Francis Boyes & Caryn Colman
City Temagami
Company Spruce Shilling Camp
Contact Chris & Verva Gaebel
City Shining Tree
Company Tatnall Camp
Contact Rolly & Linda Lebrun
City Wawa
Company The Outpost Lodge
Contact Jim & Ann Kehoe
City Thessalon
Company Voyageur Wilderness Programme Ltd.
Contact Jos & Nancy Savoie Guy & Lea
City Atikokan
Company Walser's McGregor Bay Camp
Contact Mary & Gary Walser
City Whitefish Falls
Company Wanapitei Wilderness Centre
Contact Shawn Hodgins
City Peterborough
Company Wawanaisa Resort
Contact Peter & Dorte Wiltmann
City Nobel-Dillon
Company Whip-Poor-Will Lodge
Contact Bruce & Jan Jameyson
City Amstein
Company White River Air/Mar Mac Lodge
Contact Don MacLachlan
City Sault Ste. Marie

Prince Edward Island

Company Outside Expeditions
Contact Bryon Howard & Shirley Wright
City North Rustico

Québec

Company Mabec Ltd.
Contact Douglas Poole
City Sept-Iles
Company Pourvoirie Aventure Pipmuacan
Contact Robert Laberge
City St. Augustin
Company Pourvoirie Daaquam "Qoapec Inc"
Contact Genevieve Poulin
City St.-Just De Breteniares
Company Pourvoirie Domaine Bazinet Inc.
Contact Robert Lupine

City Contrecoeur
Company Two Moons Lodge
Contact Jack Vanderdonk
City Aucune Laniel

Saskatchewan

Company Camp Grayling
Contact Margy Michel & Ed White
City Saskatoon
Company Campeau Guiding & Outfitting
Contact Alvin J. Campeau
City Carragana
Company Carriere's Camp
Contact Freda & John V. Carriere
City Cumberland House
Company Clearwater Raft Tours
Contact
City Meadow Lake
Company Craig's Place - Outfitters
Contact Dorothy & Craig Osborne
City Carrot River
Company Crystal Lodge
Contact John & Lenora Midgett
City Big River
Company Darsana Lodge
Contact Carl & Marg Boychuk
City Beauval
Company Deschambault Lake Resort
Contact Twylla Newton
City Prince Albert
Company Elks Hills Holiday Ranch
Contact Leo & Erna Oestreicher
City Lloydminster
Company Horse Creek Vacation Farm
Contact Ruby Elford
City McCord
Company Johnson's Resort
Contact Paul
City Pierceland
Company Ministikwan Lodge
Contact Dave Werner
City Loon Lake
Company Mistik Lodge
Contact Gary Carriere
City Cumberland House
Company Paull River Wilderness Camp
Contact Wayne Galloway
City Holbein
Company Pierceland Outfitters
Contact Zane Pikowicz
City Pierceland
Company Rainbow Lodge
Contact Rick & Ricky Lawrence
City Meath Park
Company Redwillow Outfitting
Contact Larry & Angela Schmitt
City Arborfield
Company RLR Outfitter
Contact Richard Rydeik
City McLean
Company Safari River Outdoors
Contact Barry Samson
City Saskatoon

Company Sask Can Outfitters
Contact Bonace Korchinski
City Saskatoon
Company Timberline Outfitting
Contact Bernard or Harvey Nokinsky
City Norquay
Company Toby's Trophy Treks
Contact Toby Coleman
City Christopher Lake
Company Torch Valley Country Retreats
Contact George & Jean Lidster
City White Fox

Yukon Territories

Company Canadian Wilderness Travel Ltd.
Contact Peter Gerasch
City Carmacks
Company Canoe North Adventures
Contact Lin Ward & Al Pace
City Orangeville, Ontario
Company Cedar & Canvas Adventures
Contact
City Whitehorse
Company Cloudberry Adventures Ltd.
Contact
City Whitehorse
Company Ecole Otter Wilderness
Contact
City Whitehorse
Company Ecosummer Yukon Expeditions
Contact Jill Pangman Joyce Majiski
City Whitehorse
Company Kanoe People Ltd.
Contact
City Whitehorse
Company Klondike River Rafting
Contact
City Dawson City
Company Macmillan River Tours
Contact
City Whitehorse
Company Nahanni River Adventures Ltd.
Contact
City Whitehorse
Company Prospect Yukon Wilderness & Watercraft
Contact Dave Goll
City Whitehorse
Company Tatshenshini Expediting Ltd.
Contact
City Whitehorse
Company Wanderlust Wilderness Adventures
Contact
City Whitehorse
Company Wolf Adventure Tours
Contact
City Whitehorse
Company Yukon Tours
Contact
City Whitehorse

Top Rated Questionnaire
Paddling Adventures

Name of your River Guide:_____

Date of Trip_____Location_____

Fully Guided Trip ☐   Day Trip ☐   Overnight Trip ☐

Was this a Family Trip where your children were actively involved in the activities?   YES ☐   No ☐

Equipment Used: Cataraft ☐   Kayak ☐ Raft ☐ Canoe ☐ Jetboat ☐   Other_____

	Outstanding	Excellent	Good	Acceptable	Poor/Inferior	Unacceptable
1. How helpful was the Outfitter/Guide with travel arrangements, dates, special accommodations, etc.?	☐	☐	☐	☐	☐	☐
2. How well did the Outfitter/Guide provide important details that better prepared you for your experience (clothing, list of "take along", difficulty of the waters, etc.)?	☐	☐	☐	☐	☐	☐
3. How would you rate the Outfitter/Guide's office skills in handling deposits, charges, reservations, returning calls before and after your trip?	☐	☐	☐	☐	☐	☐
4. How would you rate the accommodations (bunk house, tent, cabin, lodge, etc.)?	☐	☐	☐	☐	☐	☐
5. How would you rate the equipment provided by the Outfitter/Guide (boats, rafts, tents, life jackets, etc.)?	☐	☐	☐	☐	☐	☐
6. How would you rate the cooking (quantity, quality and cleanliness of the service)?	☐	☐	☐	☐	☐	☐
7. How would you rate your Outfitter/Guide's Attitude — Politeness — Disposition?	☐	☐	☐	☐	☐	☐
8. How would you rate your Outfitter/Guide's knowledge of the river?	☐	☐	☐	☐	☐	☐
9. How would you rate your Outfitter/Guide's ability to read the water?	☐	☐	☐	☐	☐	☐
10. How would you rate your Guide's skills in operating the raft/boat?	☐	☐	☐	☐	☐	☐

11. How would you rate your Outfitter/Guide's proficiency in teaching boating skills and safety? .... ☐ ☐ ☐ ☐ ☐ ☐

12. How would you rate your Outfitter/Guide's respect toward the river environment? .... ☐ ☐ ☐ ☐ ☐ ☐

13. How would you rate the quality of the different activities offered during your trip? .... ☐ ☐ ☐ ☐ ☐ ☐

14. How would you rate the overall quality of your river experience? .... ☐ ☐ ☐ ☐ ☐ ☐

15. How would you rate the skills and attitude of the staff overall? .... ☐ ☐ ☐ ☐ ☐ ☐

GOOD FAIR POOR

16. How would you describe the weather conditions? .... ☐ ☐ ☐

17. Did the Outfitter/Guide accurately represent the overall quality of your experience (quality of waters, activities, accommodations, etc.)?.............. ☐ YES ☐ No

18. Did you provide the Outfitter/Guide with truthful statements regarding your personal needs, your skills and your expectations?........................... ☐ YES ☐ No

19. Would you use this Outdoor Professional/Business again?....................... ☐ YES ☐ No

20. Would you recommend this Outdoor Professional/Business to others?..... ☐ YES ☐ No

Comments: _____
_____
_____
_____
_____
_____
_____
_____
_____
_____
_____
_____
_____
_____
_____
_____
_____

Will you permit Picked-By-You to use your name and comments in our book(s)? ☐ YES ☐ No

Signature_____

Photo Credits

Guides and Outfitters by Boat Type

 Canoe

Alaska Fish & Trails Unlimited
Bill Dvorak Kayak & Rafting Exp.
Canoe North Adventures
Canyon R.E.O.
Clearwater River Company
Earth River Expeditions
Kittatinny Canoes
Middle Earth Expeditions
Nahanni Wilderness Adventures
Outside Expeditions
Sheltowee Trace Outfitters
Sheri Griffith Expeditions
Unicorn Rafting Expeditions
Warren River Expeditions
Wild Rockies Tours

Northwest Voyageurs
O.A.R.S. Outdoor Adventure River
  Specialists
Outdoor Ventures
Rawhide Outfitters
River Travel Center
Solitude River Trips
Tightlines
Wapiti River Guides
Western Waters and Woods

 Jet Boat

Hells Canyon Adventures
Rawhide Outfitters
Warren River Expeditions
Western Waters and Woods

 Cataraft

Canyon Cats
Canyon R.E.O.
Earth River Expeditions
I.R.I.E. Rafting Company
Mild to Wild Rafting
Moser's Idaho Adventures
Northwest Voyageurs
Outdoor Ventures
Rawhide Outfitters
Turtle River Rafting Company

 Kayak K1

Bill Dvorak Kayak & Rafting Exp.
Mountain River Tour
O.A.R.S. Outdoor Adventure River
  Specialists
Southwind Kayak Center, Inc.
Spirit of Alaska Wilderness Adventures
Warren River Expeditions

 Dory/McKenzie

Bill Dvorak Kayak & Rafting Exp.
Canyon Cats
Clearwater River Company
Ewing's Whitewater
Grand Canyon Dories
Middle Fork River Tours
Moser's Idaho Adventures

 Kayak K2

Bill Dvorak Kayak & Rafting Exp.
Mountain River Tours

Guides and Outfitters by Boat Type

Inflatable Kayak

Bill Dvorak Kayak & Rafting Exp.
Canyon Cats
Canyon R.E.O.
Chinook Whitewater
Earth River Expeditions
Ewing's Whitewater
Headwaters River Company
Idaho Afloat
I.R.I.E. Rafting Company
Kittatinny Canoes
Living Waters Recreation
Middle Fork River Tours
Mild to Wild Rafting
Moser's Idaho Adventures
Mountain River Tour
Northwest Voyageurs
O.A.R.S. Outdoor Adventure River
   Specialists
Ocoee Outdoors
Outdoor Ventures
Peer's Snake River Rafting
Redline River Adventures
River Travel Center
Rocky Mountain River Tours
Sheltowee Trace Outfitters
Sheri Griffith Expeditions
Silver Cloud Expeditions
Solitude River Trips
Tightlines
Turtle River Rafting Company
Unicorn Rafting Expeditions
Wapiti River Guides
Warren River Expeditions
Wildwater Expeditions Unlimited

Sea Kayak

Bill Dvorak Kayak & Rafting Exp.
Earth River Expeditions
Outdoor Ventures
Outside Expeditions
River Travel Center
Southwind Kayak Center, Inc.
Spirit of Alaska Wilderness Adventures

Raft (paddle-oar)

Aggipah River Trips
Alaska Fish & Trails Unlimited
Bill Dvorak Kayak & Rafting Exp.
Canyon Cats
Canyon R.E.O.
Chinook Whitewater
DownStream River Runners Inc.
Earth River Expeditions
Ewing's Whitewater
Grand Canyon Dories
Headwaters River Company
Hells Canyon Adventures
Idaho Afloat
I.R.I.E. Rafting Company
Kittatinny Canoes
Living Waters Recreation
Middle Earth Expeditions
Middle Fork River Tours
Mild to Wild Rafting
Moser's Idaho Adventures
Mountain River Tour
Nahanni Wilderness Adventures
Northwest Voyageurs
O.A.R.S. Outdoor Adventure River
   Specialists
Ocoee Outdoors
Outdoor Ventures
Peer's Snake River Rafting
Pine Creek Outfitters
Rawhide Outfitters
Redline River Adventures
River Travel Center
Rocky Mountain River Tours
Sheltowee Trace Outfitters
Sheri Griffith Expeditions
Silver Cloud Expeditions
Solitude River Trips
Tightlines
Turtle River Rafting Company
Unicorn Rafting Expeditions
Wapiti River Guides
Warren River Expeditions
Western Waters and Woods
Whitewater Voyageurs

Guides and Outfitters by River Difficulty

 Class 1

Aggipah River Trips
Bill Dvorak Kayak & Rafting Exp.
Canoe North Adventures
Canyon Cats
Canyon R.E.O.
Chinook Whitewater
Clearwater River Company
DownStream River Runners Inc.
Earth River Expeditions
Headwaters River Company
Hells Canyon Adventures
Kittatinny Canoes
Living Waters Recreation
Middle Earth Expeditions
Middle Fork River Tours
Mild to Wild Rafting
Moser's Idaho Adventures
Mountain River Tour
Nahanni Wilderness Adventures
Northwest Voyageurs
O.A.R.S. Outdoor Adventure River
   Specialists
Outdoor Ventures
Outside Expeditions
Peer's Snake River Rafting
Pine Creek Outfitters
Redline River Adventures
River Travel Center
Sheri Griffith Expeditions
Silver Cloud Expeditions
Southwind Kayak Center, Inc.
Tightlines
Turtle River Rafting Company
Unicorn Rafting Expeditions
Wapiti River Guides
Warren River Expeditions
Western Waters and Woods
Whitewater Voyageurs
Wild Rockies Tours
Wildwater Expeditions Unlimited

 Class 2

Aggipah River Tours
Bill Dvorak Kayak & Rafting Exp.
Canoe North Adventures
Canyon Cats
Canyon R.E.O.
Chinook Whitewater
Clearwater River Company
Earth River Expeditions
Headwaters River Company
Hells Canyon Adventures
I.R.I.E. Rafting Company
Kittatinny Canoes
Living Waters Recreation
Middle Earth Expeditions
Middle Fork River Tours
Mild to Wild Rafting
Moser's Idaho Adventures
Mountain River Tour
Nahanni Wilderness Adventures
Northwest Voyageurs
O.A.R.S. Outdoor Adventure River
   Specialists
Ocoee Outdoors
Outdoor Ventures
Outside Expeditions
Peer's Snake River Rafting
Pine Creek Outfitters
Rawhide Outfitters
Redline River Adventures
River Travel Center
Sheri Griffith Expeditions
Silver Cloud Expeditions
Southwind Kayak Center, Inc.
Tightlines
Turtle River Rafting Company
Unicorn Rafting Expeditions
Wapiti River Guides
Warren River Expeditions
Western Waters and Woods
Whitewater Voyageurs
Wild Rockies Tours
Wildwater Expeditions Unlimited

Guides and Outfitters by River Difficulty

Class 3

Aggipah River Trips
Bill Dvorak Kayak & Rafting Exp.
Canoe North Adventures
Canyon Cats
Canyon R.E.O.
Chinook Whitewater
DownStream River Runners Inc.
Earth River Expeditions
Ewing's Whitewater
Grand Canyon Dories
Headwaters River Company
Hells Canyon Adventures
Idaho Afloat
I.R.I.E. Rafting Company
Kittatinny Canoes
Living Waters Recreation
Middle Earth Expeditions
Middle Fork River Tours
Mild to Wild Rafting
Moser's Idaho Adventures
Mountain River Tour
Nahanni Wilderness Adventures
Northwest Voyageurs
O.A.R.S. Outdoor Adventure River
    Specialists
Ocoee Outdoors
Outdoor Ventures
Outside Expeditions
Peer's Snake River Rafting
Pine Creek Outfitters
Rawhide Outfitters
Redline River Adventures
River Travel Center
Sheltowee Trace Outfitters
Sheri Griffith Expeditions
Silver Cloud Expeditions
Tightlines
Turtle River Rafting
Unicorn Rafting Expeditions
Wapiti River Guides
Warren River Expeditions
Western Waters and Woods
Whitewater Voyageurs
Wild Rockies Tours
Wildwater Expeditions Unlimited

Class 4

Aggipah River Trips
Bill Dvorak Kayak & Rafting Exp.
Canyon Cats
Canyon R.E.O.
Chinook Whitewater
Earth River Expeditions
Ewing's Whitewater
Grand Canyon Dories
Headwaters River Company
Idaho Afloat
I.R.I.E. Rafting Company
Living Waters Recreation
Middle Fork River Tours
Mild to Wild Rafting
Moser's Idaho Adventures
Mountain River Tour
Northwest Voyageurs
O.A.R.S. Outdoor Adventure River
    Specialists
Ocoee Outdoors
Outdoor Ventures
Peer's Snake River Rafting
Rawhide Outfitters
Redline River Adventures
River Travel Center
Rocky Mountain River Tours
Sheltowee Trace Outfitters
Sheri Griffith Expeditions
Tightlines
Turtle River Rafting Company
Unicorn Rafting Expeditions
Warren River Expeditions
Whitewater Voyageurs
Wildwater Expeditions Unlimited

Guides and Outfitters by River Difficulty/ Schools

Class 5

Bill Dvorak Kayak & Rafting Exp.
Canyon R.E.O.
Earth River Expeditions
Grand Canyon Dories
LivingWaters Recreation
Middle Fork River Tours
Mild to Wild Rafting
Mountain River Tour
Northwest Voyageurs
O.A.R.S. Outdoor Adventure River
    Specialists
Outdoor Ventures
Redline River Adventures
River Travel Center
Rocky Mountain River Tours
Sheltowee Trace Outfitters
Sheri Griffith Expeditions
Turtle River Raftin Company
Unicorn Rafting Expeditions
Whitewater Voyageurs
Wildwater Expeditions Unlimited

School, River Raft and Kayak

Bill Dvorak Kayak & Rafting Exp.
DownStream River Runners, Inc.
Earth River Expeditons
Kittatinny Canoes
Middle Fork River Tours
Mountain River Tours
Northwest Voyageurs
O.A.R.S. Outdoor Adventure River
    Specialists
Outdoor Ventures
Redline River Adventures
Southwind Kayak Center, Inc.
Turtle River Rafting Company
Warren River Expeditions

Class 6

Northwest Voyageurs
Redline River Adventures
Sheltowee Trace Outfitters

Guides and Outfitters by State

Guides and Outfitters by State

Guides and Outfitters by Province

Canada

Alphabetical Index by Company Name

About the Editor

Maurizio (Maurice) Valerio received a Doctoral degree Summa Cum Laude in Natural Science, majoring in Animal Behaviour, from the University of Parma (Italy) in 1981, and a Master of Arts degree in Zoology from the University of California, Berkeley in 1984.

He is a rancher, a writer and a devoted outdoorsman who decided to live with the wild animals that he cherishes so much in the Wallowa Mountains of Northeast Oregon. He has traveled extensively in the Old and New World, for more than 25 years. He is dedicated to preserving everyone's individual right of a respectful, knowledgeable and diversified use of our Outdoor Resources.